RUNNING STORIES

EDITED BY JERRY LOCKSPEISER & ANDREW ROBERTS

Running Stories
ISBN 978-1-8383764-0-6

Cover illustration and book design
by Andrew Roberts

Published by Hightale
London, 2021

CONTENTS

THE STORIES

RUNNING GOT ME THROUGH

RUNNING JOURNEYS

RACING TALES

THE COMPETITIVE SPIRIT

IT'S ABOUT OTHER PEOPLE TOO

IT MAKES ME FEEL SO GOOD

TWO CONTRASTING VIEWS

THE RUNNING CHARITY

ACKNOWLEDGEMENTS

ABOUT THIS BOOK

This book is about people who run. Their reasons for running and the role it plays in their lives are as varied as they are.

A few are very fast and run to win; some run to build confidence, prove a point, deal with a health problem, make friends or help others; many luxuriate in the feeling of wellness it brings. For a number, running enabled escape from the very worst of personal circumstances. Every story is as unique as the person who wrote it.

When we had the idea for a book of running stories, we sent out a call for contributions to our network of friends, family, running clubs and other running organisations. They in turn passed the message on. The call produced a much greater response than we had anticipated. Clearly running matters to a lot of people, many of whom are keen to share their experience.

We asked people to write about something special to them associated with running. For some this was a single focus, such as an event, a place, or a person; for others it was how they felt; for several it was a combination.

The 88 short stories here were chosen for their individual interest and their diversity when combined. The photographs of the storyteller complement and amplify the written words.

We have organised the stories into six broad themes:

RUNNING GOT ME THROUGH

Running is perhaps most powerful when helping people to overcome grief and loss, deal with physical adversity, or escape from dire personal situations. These stories show how crucial it can be.

RUNNING JOURNEYS

These are personal journeys, from beginning as a child in an Ibo village to a first run on a hill in Sheffield; from enjoying one of the best runs on the planet to trying to lose weight; from running with diabetes to running with children. And many others.

RACING TALES

From parkrun to ultra-marathon, these stories are all about races. That's where the similarity ends. Each person describes their event from a different angle, every experience is unique.

THE COMPETITIVE SPIRIT

Winning medals or achieving records is the theme in these stories – including from people in their 70s.

IT'S ABOUT OTHER PEOPLE TOO

Making new friends, finding love, raising funds for charity, guiding a blind runner, coaching, or being coached – these are some of the ways other people impact the runner's experience.

IT MAKES ME FEEL SO GOOD

This features stories about wellness, joy, mental health, freedom, self-confidence, self-belief and running in nature. And, in one case, because running takes less time than swimming.

We hope that this book will appeal across the community of runners and beyond, especially to people thinking about running for the first time. The chapter **Questions new runners ask** seeks to answer 10 things new runners – or those thinking about running – often wonder about. We have referenced stories in the book to illustrate each answer, because there is no better way to explain than by using the experience of others.

Among the many inspiring stories are those from young people who have been helped by **The Running Charity**. This small but essential organisation uses running as the vehicle to help homeless young people overcome their personal difficulties and rebuild their lives. We are delighted to donate 100% of our revenue from this book to The Running Charity. Co-founder Alex Eagle describes their work on page 172.

We trust the stories in this book will strike a chord with you. If you do not currently run, perhaps they will give you confidence to put your trainers on and head out of the front door. If you are a runner, perhaps you will see yourself in the words of others.

Jerry Lockspeiser
Andrew Roberts

QUESTIONS NEW RUNNERS ASK

Thinking of running? Just starting?
Ten tips to help you love it.

1. CAN I RUN? ME?

Yes, yes, yes, and yes. You can. For sure. See the stories by **Sarah Price** (page 60), **Mel Heale** (page 42), and **Rahema Mamodo** (page 142) for people filled with self-doubt who put one foot forward and have never looked back. Your age, shape and speed don't matter. Just take the first step and the rest will follow.

Don't let doubt build up in your mind. If it's already there, tell it to get lost. Running is the most natural thing – look at kids. It is as natural as breathing. It is your right.

No one is watching you. If someone sees you by chance in the street or the park, they don't care what you are doing. In fact, they may be envious, wishing they could do it too. Which of course they can. So, why not tell them?

If you feel it's easier to start running with a friend, ask around. Most people who already run will be pleased to help; people who want to start, like you, may welcome sharing the dare. See question 7 too.

2. DOES IT MATTER WHAT I WEAR?

Craig McMurrough (page 137) runs marathons dressed as a giant ovary to raise funds for charity. If he can run in that, anything is possible! For people who are new to running and just want to try

it out, a T-shirt or sweatshirt, shorts or leggings, and a pair of comfortable trainers will get you out the door. Then if you decide running is going to be a regular part of your life getting properly kitted out is worthwhile, helping your comfort and preventing injury. Experienced runners, especially those competing in races, often spend time and money choosing specific gear.

Shoes are the most important part of what to wear as your feet take the strain first. If you decide you like running and it becomes a regular thing it's worth getting a pair of running shoes that suit your feet. Most independent running shops can assess what is best for you.

Next get some clothes that are designed for running. Avoid cotton tops because they absorb sweat and get heavy. Lightweight breathable sports tops that 'wick' sweat away from your body are best, so you feel lighter and fresher.

A decent sports bra is a necessity for most women runners.

3. DO I NEED TO STRETCH AND WARM UP BEFORE I RUN?

Yes. Many people don't, but there is a simple logic in why it's a good idea. Running puts extra strain on many parts of the body, and if they are not prepared, they may decide to go on strike. Injuries can result. Stretching gives advance warning of what is to come, easing different parts of the body into a ready state; warming up gets the blood flowing and the muscles better prepared for the increased demands. A brisk walk or light jog before running is a good start. As the humorous tale by **Peter Stafford-Bow** (page 52) describes, it's a very good idea to stretch after running too.

4. HOW FAST, FAR AND OFTEN SHOULD I RUN?

This depends on your level of fitness when you start running. For someone who has not been undertaking any sport or exercise, our advice is take it easy and increase distance, speed, and frequency very gradually. It's impossible to do too little or go too slowly at first. This allows your body to adapt well, and it's a great feeling to do a little bit more each time. We find that getting those trainers on two or three times a week helps mental and physical progression more than a single weekly blast. **Tom Albrighton** (page 56) describes the gradual progress in his running journey.

5. DO I NEED TO EAT OR DRINK?

NHS advice is to allow about three hours after a main meal before exercise; that eating a light, easily digestible higher carbohydrate snack such as porridge or a banana an hour before may help performance and recovery; and that you shouldn't need to eat during exercise of an hour or less in duration.

Our experience is that running when you feel hungry isn't great, so something light and healthy beforehand works well. But this is a very individual thing. **Helen Worsfold** (page 90) experienced the potential pitfalls of eating during a very long run.

Common advice on fluids is to make sure you have drunk enough water to be well hydrated before starting to run, and to consume 100-150ml every 20 minutes (about the amount in a standard wine glass). People vary in how much water they feel like drinking – we are at the low consumption end of the spectrum – and it's uncomfortable if you feel it sloshing around inside you. Our advice is to drink a little water at the very first sign of thirst, or even before. Don't leave it until you feel very thirsty or you will already be finding it harder to run.

6. WILL I LOSE WEIGHT?

It's very likely but depends what else you do apart from running! Losing weight means burning more calories than you consume. Running is a great way to burn calories as it requires many muscles to work together. So if you don't go to the pub after running and drink lots of alcohol, eat lots of crisps and swallow a packet of chocolates on the way home, running can contribute significantly to weight loss in the context of a healthy lifestyle. See the extraordinary story told by **Lisa Butler** (page 34).

7. HOW CAN I FIND OTHER PEOPLE TO RUN WITH?

The three easiest ways are to ask friends or colleagues who run, or who don't but you think might like to try it too; to search online for your local running club – the majority are super friendly and for people of all levels, not just the fast guys; or go to your local parkrun on a Saturday morning – the brilliant walking, jogging, running 5k for absolutely everyone. It's free and easy to make friends.

Carole O'Leary (page 134) describes starting the Coffee Runners in London, one of many such friendly groups throughout the country; **Charlie Thuillier** (page 128) found love at his running club; **Stacey Tasker** (page 122) found true friends through parkrun.

8. AM I TOO OLD TO RUN?

We could ask, are you too old to breathe? This book has many stories from older runners – by which we mean people aged 60 plus. **Alex Rotas** (page 115) describes how she photographs amazing older athletes, **Roger Sawtell** (page 68) tells how he started running aged 92, while **Anne Dockery** (page 100) went from having a serious lung condition to World Champion aged 70. You are never too old.

9. WILL I FEEL PAIN?

In our experience there are two kinds of pain – effort pain and injury pain.

Effort pain is good pain – it shows you are making demands of yourself. It is temporary and stops when you stop running. Injury pain is bad. It's usually, but not always, easy to tell them apart, but if in doubt stop. Some runners think they can "run through pain" when injured. Our physiotherapists don't recommend this as it is likely to aggravate the injury. **Richard Price** (page 82) describes his injury treatment and it's almost too painful to read!

Effort pain is the feeling that what you are doing is hard – because it's new and you aren't used to it, or because what you are doing is very demanding for you (some things are always very demanding for everyone, like the last few miles of a marathon). Your muscles might feel a bit stiff afterwards, which is normal. The more you run, the more they adapt, the less stiff they should feel. The first few times you run you may have a prickly sensation on your skin, probably your chest. It goes after a few runs as your body adapts. A childhood experience taught **Michelle Mortimer** (page 64) about effort pain and why it's OK.

10. SHOULD I SET A GOAL?

It's entirely up to you. Many of us find it easier to be motivated if we know what we are trying to achieve, whether it is jogging 100 metres or running a marathon. It doesn't matter how small the goal is, it's your goal. When you have achieved it, you may want to set a new one that is slightly harder. As with running itself, goals are best done in sensible and achievable progression, not mad leaps. Many people say that to avoid injury and build a strong running base it is wise not to increase distance by more than 10% each week.

We love the Couch to 5k programme for new runners. It's free to download and involves getting from your couch to running 5k (3.1 miles) in nine weeks, starting in week one by running for a minute, then walking, then running and so on. It's a brilliant example of setting an achievable goal, with all the satisfaction that brings. Running clubs and groups often use it.

Many of the stories here are about people's goals. From **Nick Bester** (page 76) running the Comrades Ultra marathon to **Joe Cancelliere** (page 111) aiming to run the distance around the world – and many less extreme objectives – people are challenging themselves. No matter what the goal, everyone starts with the first step.

These 10 tips come from our experiences and those of others we know. We are not medical or sports professionals, so please get qualified advice if you need it.

RUNNING WORDS & PHRASES

Seeing the crowd barriers for a race in central London a few years ago, I asked the security guard what the event was. "It's the London 10k marathon" he replied. And why not? Runners will know that a **10k** is a race of 10 kilometres, whereas a **marathon** is a race of **42.2 kilometres (26.2 miles)**. It cannot be both. To the security guard, however, the race was simply long.

For the non-runner, distances, times and gradings can be a fog. This book is about the runners themselves, not geeky information, and contains a very limited range of terms and abbreviations. Nonetheless, a few appear from time to time.

The most common are distances. For the most part these are what they say – a **5k**, or 5km, is 5 kilometres (which is 3.1 miles). Races on road or cross country in the UK are talked about in kilometres or miles – common distances are **5k** and **10k**, and the longer **10** and **20 miles**. However, a 5k run on a track is called **5000 metres**, and a 10k is called **10,000 metres**. Same distance, different conditions, different way of referring to it.

Unsurprisingly, a **half marathon** is exactly half of the full marathon distance – it is **21.1 kilometres, 13.1 miles**. However, there is no specific definition of the length of an ultramarathon. Any distance further than the marathon's 42.2k, 26.2 miles, is called an **ultramarathon**. They can be **50 kilometres, 100 kilometres, 100 miles** or you name it. All of these are mega

distances to run, but if someone has run an ultramarathon you can find out just how crazy they are by asking how far it was.

The surge of interest in running in the last few years has been inspired by people's desire for better mental and physical health. Several of these stories mention two popular ways people are pursuing these goals.

The first is **parkrun**, the **free 5k run**, walk, or jog every Saturday morning – pandemics permitting – started in 2004 by Paul Sinton-Hewitt in Bushy Park, London. It now takes place in 2000 locations across 22 countries. Parkrun is about wellbeing not speed. Paul has said how pleased he is when the average parkrun finishing time gets slower.

The second is **Couch to 5k** (or C25K), mentioned in the **Questions new runners ask** section. Originally created in 1996 by Josh Clark, the UK NHS has a downloadable programme that does what it says in the name – gets the non-runner from sitting on their couch to being able to complete a 5K in nine weeks. Based on a very gradual build up, with alternating days of running and rest, it is hugely effective and beneficial.

Some faster running contributors mention **reps** and **bpm**. Reps stands for repetitions, which, as it suggests, is about repeating a time or distance, with a recovery interval between the runs – so this kind of training is either called repetition training or interval training. Its purpose is to develop the person's ability to run faster and faster for longer, the structure of running and intervals varying according to the runner's specific objective.

Heart rate (or pulse) as measured in bpm – beats per minute – can be used to guide effort when running, both for people with health issues and as the focus of a training plan. The runner needs to wear a heart rate monitor, either a chest strap linked to a fitness tracker or sports watch, or one of these with a built-in monitor.

Runners trying to improve their time aim for a **PB** – a Personal Best for that distance. Some countries, including the USA and France, call it a PR – Personal Record. Whichever it is, runners trying to achieve a quicker time for a specific distance will choose fast, flat courses where possible. For the most competitive runners and their coaches, the **Power of 10** website (PO10) is a huge database listing every official race a runner has done, with rankings by event and age.

The **Age Grading** system is a fun way to see how you are performing compared to others of your age and sex. Taking these into account, Age Grading produces a percentage score for a runner's time comparative to the world best of the same category. Scores above 90% are said to show a runner of international standard, from 80-90% of national competition standard, 70-80% regional and 60-70% local. People usually slow down as they get older, but if they perform relatively well their age grading percentage may rise. Using the Age Grading system can be motivating for older runners and allows someone to monitor their performance at different ages. For example, someone who runs a time that produces a 65% score age 35, then runs a slower time for the same distance at age 55 that produces 70%, is doing relatively better when older.

ADRIAN KERR·ADRIAN LOBB·ALEX ROTAS·ALUN LUCAS·ANDREA SANDERS-REECE·ANDREAS NORDGREN·ANDY FOSTER·ANGELA SMITH·ANNE BROMLEY·ANNE DOCKERY·ANNIE TRIHAN·ATSUKO WHITEHOUSE·BARBARA PRESTON·BECCY LOCKSPEISER·CAROLE O'LEARY·CAROLINE GILBY·CELESTINE AGBO·CHARLIE THUILLIER·CHRISTIAN WOLMAR·CIARAN THAPAR·CLYDE WILLIAMSON·CORY WHARTON-MALCOLM·CRAIG MCMURROUGH·DARREN EVANS·DAVID CHALEEN·DAVID SPENCER·DIANA VALK·DR JOHN ETHERINGTON·FIONA ENGLISH·FRANKIE LYNCH·GABRIELLE PELTER·GRACE WU·HELEN HALL·HELEN WORSFOLD·HUGH BALFOUR·IAN JONES·JACQUIE MILLER·IAN SMITH·JERRY CAREY·JOE ANTHONY·JOE BEST·JOE CANCELLIERE·JOE OGBONNA·JOE SMITH·JOHN & PAUL SMITH·JOSE SANCHEZ ALONSO-MARDONES·JULIA JAMES·KATI JAEGER·KATSURA ISOBE·KELLY LANGFORD·KITTY STEWART·LILY LANG·LISA BUTLER·LIZZIE CURRIE·MALCOLM BERESFORD·MEL HEALE·MICHELLE MORTIMER·MIRY MAYER·MOHAMUD AADAN·NEIL BRADSHAW·NEIL JOHNS·NICK BESTER·NIKKI LAKIN·OLIVIA KILMARTIN·PETER STAFFORD-BOW·PHIL BRADBURN·PHILIPPA PERRY·RAHEMA MAMODO·RAUL KHARBANDA·RHYSS MACKAY·RICHARD PRICE·RICHIE THOMAS·ROGER SAWTELL·RYAN FRIEL·SALLY RAMSDEN·SANDY WALL·SAOIRSE SMITH·SARAH PRICE·SARAH WATSON·SEYFU JAMAAL·SID WILLS·STACEY TASKER·SUE RESSEL·TOM ALBRIGHTON·TOM ANTHONY·TOM BARTLETT·VIC SHIRLEY

RUNNING GOT ME THROUGH

I FEEL SO GRATEFUL
GABRIELLE PELTER

For me running has never been about times, distances, races, medals or improving my PB. I know this sounds crazy to most people who define themselves as runners, I've been told this on more than a few occasions! Why on earth do I run then, if I'm not training for my next big race or looking to beat my personal records?

WILL I BE ABLE TO WALK WHEN I WAKE UP TOMORROW?

When I was 24, I was diagnosed with Multiple Sclerosis (MS), a devastating autoimmune degenerative condition which has changed my life forever. One of the main characteristics of having MS is that I have no idea what the future will bring. Uncertainty is rife. Will I be able to walk when I wake up tomorrow? After already experiencing a previous episode of MS-related sight loss, could I wake up again unable to see? Will I be in a wheelchair in the future? Will I still be able to dance at the Notting Hill Carnival, which is my favourite thing ever? Will I be able to be a good mother? I live with these fears every day.

For me, running is about being in the moment, letting go of some of those fears – at least momentarily – and feeling so grateful that I am able to run that day. Even if I'm experiencing extreme fatigue (different to tiredness – it literally feels like running through sand dunes or treacle) or I can't run very fast, I run. I run because

I can, and I'm grateful for that. I run with a smile on my face even when my body doesn't feel good and is viciously protesting. I run listening to my most joyous music. I enjoy every bead of sweat on my body, every gust of breeze on my face, every flower blossom, every cute child or dog I pass, taking in my surroundings to the fullest.

GOING AS FAST AS MY BODY PERMITS THAT DAY

When I run, I listen to my body, going as fast as my body permits that day, and I try not to beat myself up too much for being 'slow', if that is what my body needs. But that's been a difficult journey. Sometimes my left leg drags or I'm in pain or I feel a bit unsteady, which can be so disheartening and demoralising and can knock my confidence right in the gut. Sometimes, I get overwhelmed with envy of other runners who can 'just run' with their 'normal' bodies and 'normal' aches and pains, as they strive for self-improvement, seemingly taking everything for granted. Believe me, I've had lots of incomplete runs with mini diversion 'cry walks' before getting a grip! However now I try not to compare myself to others and focus on myself and my own personal motives for running – gratitude, joy, and my emotional wellbeing.

I really enjoy volunteering at running events in the community, for example the local annual half marathon and 10k events.

I've become an expert 'running cheerleader', encouraging every runner, staying on to support, right until the final few. But I'm often reluctant to sign up to running events or races myself, because of the looming 'what if' in the back of my mind: what if my body does not 'work' properly on race day? I feel like I don't need the added pressure.

JUST HOPING THAT I'D BE ABLE TO ENJOY THE RUN

Despite this, I've completed two 10k events, both of which were such a huge achievement for me. I was so nervous both times, approaching the start line still thinking, 'there is no way I can do this'

and 'what am I doing here with all these runners?' I was just hoping both times that my legs would work with me, not against me – as I do almost every time I run – and that I'd be able to enjoy the run.

What's next for me? I choose not to look too far ahead, but to just take each day as it comes. When I have been for a run, even if it was a difficult one, I try to focus on being proud of myself. The main priority for me is showing up and getting out there, running when I can and being grateful for every step.

So, you may well see me steadily running out in a local park or on the streets, joyfully listening to my soca music, smiling and dancing – well, at least in my head!

I'M STILL RUNNING
ALUN LUCAS

We lost a child to a late miscarriage. We lost a marriage. I lost a job to 'low mood due to multiple life events' as the doctor phrased it. I was lucky. She is a fabulous doctor and she went the extra mile, referring me to a local counselling service, The Cogwheel Trust in Cambridge, as well as the NHS mental health services. I saw an excellent counsellor at The Cogwheel Trust; a man who enjoyed rugby and beer and who kept asking me 'Who are you?' I realised I didn't know. I had spent my life jumping through hoops for other people. I had fantastic friends and a loving, supportive family. A wonderful godfather and his wife. And my children.

On New Year's Eve, I met a gorgeous woman. We went birdwatching; I saw a goldeneye for the first time. Her partner had committed suicide. She was planning to do Run Every Day January to fundraise for Mind. I joined in.

COULD I RUN EVERY DAY FOR A YEAR, I WONDERED?

At the end of a month of running every day, I felt so much better I kept going. Could I run every day for a year, I wondered? Probably not, I thought. Fundraise for The Cogwheel Trust and the Campaign Against Living Miserably, CALM. Gorgeous woman said she'd buy pizza if I did.

Beer was involved. I run with the Hash House Harriers. Meet at a pub, go for a non-competitive run, return to pub,

drink beer, and enjoy the 'craic'. He said "Well it's got to be 2019 miles hasn't it? You're finishing in 2019, so it's got to be 2019 miles." "Yes." I replied. "It's got to be." "And you run ultramarathons?" "Yes, I do." "So, it has to be an ultramarathon a month doesn't it?" More beer. "Yes."

YOU'LL NOT BE RUNNING FOR A FEW DAYS

What a fantastic year. Running. 2019 miles. 12 ultramarathons. And adventures in Bessie the Campervan. The Sandlings Way over a weekend – thanks to the landlord and landlady who entertained me on the Friday night! Completing the route of the 'Apocalypse' in Shropshire that had previously beaten me – thanks for the kind words man not on a motorcycle! Thank you to the doctor who said "You'll not be running for a few days" as I entered Accident and Emergency after a bizarre adventure in which I got run over by my own campervan, and then – in response to my tears – explained in detail how I might – just – be able to do it. And did. Thanks for rescuing me... again, sis!

Thanks to the wonderful friends who supported, fed, and watered me along The South Downs Way. How did Bessie get locked in that car park? Thanks to those who set her free! Superb day with great friends at the Stour Valley Path Ultra. Several superb days at Endurancelife Ultras – challenging but fun – and a great bunch of people.

I FEEL VERY WELL

A remarkable screening of the brave and moving film 'Evelyn' – and a brave, big hearted and engaging sister who enabled an auditorium of people affected by suicide to talk about it. And huge thanks to all those generous donors who sponsored me. The memories and stories overflow. And I kept thinking "I feel well." Some weeks later, I'd think "I feel very well."

Again. And I knew I felt better than I had the time before. On the Darent Valley Path. On the Icknield Way Path. Could that keep happening? Surely that recovery has to 'top out' – to reach a pinnacle – the summit of one's life? Not yet. Fingers crossed.

And I am still running.

Every day.

RUNNING AWAY FROM SPICE
RHYSS MACKAY

I became homeless at the age of 18 in Newcastle after family problems forced me to leave home. I moved into a Salvation Army hostel, where I began to suffer from severe depression and anxiety. Within a month of being homeless I was introduced to legal highs. I soon became hooked on Spice as it helped me sleep and forget my situation. Over the next few years, I was constantly being moved between different hostels. I slept rough on the streets for over 12 months and was sent to prison for the first time, for shoplifting. During the six years I was homeless my mental health really suffered and I attempted suicide 14 times.

In January 2015, an outreach team found me in a doorway in the city centre suffering from hypothermia and got me a place in emergency accommodation. I lived there for a year before being asked to leave for persistent rule-breaking and bringing drugs onto the premises. I was then sent back to prison for three months before moving back into the hostel. I managed to stop offending but was still struggling with addiction. Over the next 12 months I tried to kick Spice on three occasions, only to relapse again.

Then, at the beginning of November 2017, The Running Charity visited the hostel. I remember it like it was yesterday. I had only been off Spice for five days and was really struggling to keep it up when George came and asked if anyone would like to go for a run in the park. It was dark and wet but for some reason I agreed to go out with him. I think it was partly because I felt bad that he had driven all the way from Manchester and nobody else was going to run with him. That was the start of my running journey. It was Guy Fawkes night and we ran for half an hour wearing head torches in Heaton Park. It was the first physical exercise I had done in around five years. The feeling was amazing.

I COULDN'T WIPE THE SMILE OFF MY FACE THAT NIGHT

However, the next day I was feeling low again and waiting to get some Spice dropped off at the hostel. I couldn't sleep. Then I saw the head-torch George had left for me and decided to run around the block to try and kill time. I ended up running for 45 minutes. I couldn't wipe the smile from my face that night.

A week later George came back, and we went running again. He suggested I try a parkrun, which I loved. This was the point I realised I was a better runner than I thought. The progression in my running and my mental health went hand in hand and I started feeling better in myself. One of the hostel support workers signed me up to volunteer at a parkrun so I was finishing my run (in the top 10 by now) then putting on a volunteer jacket to scan the barcodes of other runners as they finished. This gave me a great feeling.

I knew by then that running could do a lot for me and I have never looked back. Looking after my physical health for

Rhyss left, cardboard Mo centre and George right

running became important so I started to distance myself from friends who were still using drugs. Friday nights became early nights instead of party nights, and over the following months my running progressed rapidly. I was now finishing in the top three and looking for my first win! The benefits were more than physical, my confidence was growing all the time too. I was making different choices and starting to believe in myself. I even went back to college.

In January 2018, I moved into my own flat. I continued to train with The Running Charity, graduating from their programme and taking part in a series of Young Ambassador training workshops. I became a Mental Health Support Volunteer with Depaul UK, the organisation that ran the hostel that helped me so much. Then following an England Athletics Run Leaders course I became a volunteer with The Running Charity and I am now the lead contact for any future programmes in the North East.

In 2019, after over a year of volunteering in the homeless sector, I was offered a full-time role at CRISIS as a Trainee Progression Coach, using my lived experience to support others and help them change their lives. This was just the opportunity I needed.

Life has continued to throw challenges my way and it hasn't always been easy, but running has given me the strength to make the right decisions where it matters most. I recommend anyone who feels flat or not as great as you hope, to try going for a run. I honestly think I wouldn't be the person I am today if I hadn't met The Running Charity.

OUT OF THE DARKNESS
JERRY CAREY

Growing up I had a troubled childhood. I was exposed to a range of abuse and violence at a very young age. I ran away from home into a world of addiction, drug abuse and vulnerability. I was put into foster care but continued to run away. I put myself into vulnerable and dangerous situations where I was taken advantage of and neglected.

This continued until my late teens when I settled with a new foster family where I no longer had access to my drugs of choice and swapped to alcohol. I ended up in various abusive relationships, but one at age 22 ruined my life and destroyed me in ways I didn't think possible. I lost everything.

During the relationship I experienced every form of abuse. I was isolated, gaslighted, manipulated, psychologically conditioned and controlled 24/7. I wasn't allowed access to my phone, friends, or family. I wasn't allowed to go anywhere alone, even inside the house. I wasn't allowed to look at or talk to anyone but him. He would find reasons to abuse me daily, even though I did everything he told me to. He'd make up impossible stories to be abusive and justify his behaviour. I was unable to sleep, eat, ask for help, or defend myself.

The relationship lasted a year until I lost a chance at being a mother and suffered greatly from many complications. I felt there was nothing more he could do to hurt me. It took a year for me to escape with the help of multiple police calls. During this time, my ex-partner began harassing and stalking me at home, at work, during appointments and online. Abusive and threatening messages and calls continued daily until he was arrested a third time. When the restriction order was put in place and the abuse stopped, I didn't know how to cope. I was suicidal, severely anxious, terrified (PTSD), depressed and alone.

AND THEN I MET THE RUNNING CHARITY

I isolated myself for three years, only leaving the house twice a month to attend medical appointments. I felt there was no hope or future for me, my world was a dark and helpless place. My psychologist referred me to Woman's Aid for a six week programme which helped clarify that I wasn't alone and that it wasn't my fault, which I needed to hear. At the end of the programme I was asked if I wanted support keeping fit. In a rare optimistic five minutes I said yes and then I met The Running Charity.

WE BEGAN WITH A WEEKLY ONE TO ONE RUN

After meeting one of the coaches we began with a weekly one to one run. In the beginning I found the distress of leaving the house extremely difficult and couldn't run more than a minute without having

fantastic support. I began training for my first race and first half marathon. This was an amazing experience and my love for running skyrocketed. Since then I've run multiple races, different distances and have 12 medals on my wall as a reminder of my achievements and just how far I've come.

RUNNING AND FITNESS HAVE CHANGED MY LIFE FOR THE BETTER

Thanks to the amazing people at The Running Charity, the wonders of running and fitness have changed my life for the better. I am no longer isolated, have control over my anxiety and depression, and have more confidence. I barely recognise the person I was two to three years ago.

THE LAST STEP TO RECOVERY AND HEALING IS HELPING OTHERS

I see a positive life and future for myself and have decided to make what I love most my new career path. I am soon to start studying to become a personal trainer so I can help others. I can't see myself doing anything else. I believe the last step to recovery and healing is helping others.

o stop. In time I was running regular 5ks and was then introduced to The Running Charity group runs. This was scary for me until I got to know everyone and saw how kind and supportive they were.

After settling into the group and attending every run I started to feel more secure and have more control over my anxiety, panic attacks and depression. I quit smoking, drinking and drugs, and had something to look forward to, a positive outlook and

A LETTER TO MY GIRL
BARBARA PRESTON

RUNNING GOT ME THROUGH

Hey Isla... I was a normal, young Scottish girl. I grew up thinking nothing of running or jogging, or why on earth anyone would do this! I went to the sick bay when I had to do any sort of running. I was chubby and shy. I thought running meant being out of breath, pain, a red face, not fun, not beautiful. I thought I would be laughed at if I ran. If I moved. It was for the girls and boys naturally built for it, the confident and popular ones.

When I went to University there was a running club which the beautiful runners went to. Those girls with the swishing ponytails and small bodies. The boys had big shoulders and big legs. These people looked like they did this easily and normally. This wasn't me. I was the shy girl, the clever girl with dimples, the girl who loved to talk, who loved books. No swishing ponytails. She wasn't one of them.

But always, this girl was a daddy's girl. She was beautiful to him. There she felt safe and beautiful. And then at the age of 26, her daddy died, suddenly and without any beauty. With no warning, love and beauty went. And she sat, without books, without laughing, without life. Until one day her friend Karen said come with me, we can walk, and we can talk.

We walked and we talked, about him, about what he meant and what I could be. And that walk became something, without any thought, something faster. It carried me along. And the old worn out everyday trainers became new, boxed trainers for people who run. A big £30 was spent.

My body went where my mind couldn't. From 20 seconds to one minute, to five minutes, to 30 minutes.

And then, my friend said, "let's run a half marathon." How? How far is that? How can I do that? I can't? How can my feet keep going that long? A lot of questions. I can't – but I did. I walked, I ran a bit, something kept me going – or someone.

I learnt that my feet could take me to a place of love. To carry the sadness of not having Grampa with me. My little feet did that. I ran when I was carrying you in my tummy. You came along with me. Here you were being carried by mummy, who felt her baby and her daddy with her, now with a sort of swishing ponytail.

And now mummy is faster, her feet and mind know that if she keeps moving, she can do so much more. And this is for you. This is how when I run, I think of you, and I think of him. It's beautiful.

Love Mummy XXX

MY SUPERHERO
ANGELA SMITH

Everyone starts running for a reason. It may be health reasons, the challenge, or perhaps it's just what you've always done.

My reason? It was all for my superhero, my Dad. He is not here in person as cancer decided to take him away from us. I lost my Dad in October 2012 and not a day goes by when I don't think about him. So many things trigger memories.

Hearing someone whistling indoors or crossing on the stairs. This is when I hear my superstitious Dad yell. Horse racing and greyhounds. Rhyl and Blackpool. Road rage and 1000 sneezes one after the other. Even a line for the toilet. These things remind me of the most important man in my life.

I had never been one for exercise. The thought of running made me want to go and hide! After losing our Dad my sister decided to run a half marathon to raise money for Macmillan Cancer Support in memory of him.

I COULD DO THIS

Of course, I went to support her and watching her and the thousand others cross the finishing line inspired me to think "I could do this."

I knew I wouldn't be jumping into half marathons, so I decided on participating in the Great Run Birmingham 10k. And of course, it would be for my Dad and raising money for Macmillan.

Needless to say, every medal I earn now is still for my superhero.

I hope I do him proud.

I WANT TO RUN FOR GB
SEYFU JAMAAL

Seyfu came to the UK to seek asylum from the political turmoil and problems in his place of birth, the Bale Province of Ethiopia.

Leaving Ethiopia, he travelled through Sudan, Libya, across the Mediterranean Sea to Italy, then across Europe to France, and finally to England.

It took Seyfu over 17 months to reach the UK, dangerously covering thousands of miles on foot. The journey was emotionally painful and often physically very difficult.

During the journey he witnessed events that were immensely traumatic for a young person to see that he found hard to comprehend, significantly affecting the formative years of his teenage life.

"The journey was tormenting, like a horror film. Experiences where you would choose to die rather than live, but that is not the option. The journey... here your existence and life are in the hands of traffickers, they choose whether you live or die.

"I witnessed people being murdered in the desert so that the traffickers could assert their authority. To scare you into submission they beat you and ransom you, buy you and sell you. It's not just me but they do it to thousands of people.

"People think slavery has been abolished. Between Sudan and Libya, we were treated as a commodity, bought and sold, bought and sold, people telling you they own you, that you are their property. You always feel captured."

Seyfu finally arrived in the UK aged just 17. The preceding four months had seen him particularly isolated, often sleeping rough and surviving very poor conditions with no support. He was overjoyed to be safe now that part of his journey was over.

Seyfu was referred to The Running Charity by the British Red Cross and it quickly became apparent that he was a talented and passionate runner, with a commitment to working hard to achieve. He was inspired by the history of international runners from Ethiopia.

The Running Charity was able to provide Seyfu with an environment where he felt welcomed, listened to, and supported.

WHEN I RUN, I AM HEALTHY, I AM HAPPY

"Running removes my stress, my mental problems, I forget, it's my remedy. When I run, I am healthy, I am happy.

"There are times you remember the problems, the journey, the traffickers but I feel safe in England. I have never felt unsafe when I have been here."

Seyfu's first road race with The Running Charity was the Oxford Half Marathon. He started with the fun runners at the back, but his speed and desire to do his best saw him blaze a path past some of the most experienced runners in the UK. Seyfu came second out of over 10,000 runners.

One of his proudest moments came nearly

a year later when he won the London Landmarks Half Marathon, beating over 14,000 runners. Seyfu has continued to improve his times with personal bests that include a 66:05 half marathon, 31:04 10km, and 14:42 5km. He is currently the UK number two for under 20s.

Seyfu has flourished within the supportive setting provided. He has formed genuine friendships, grown in confidence, and become a leader in The Running Charity sessions, supporting other young runners that are referred into our community, fast or slow.

Asked why he continues to run with the Charity when his running is elite level, and he now runs and is captain for his local club, Seyfu said: "I liked the commitment, the desire to help people, your friendship is something I never want to lose, I feel cared for and appreciated. The Running Charity is my family, without them I would be at home alone and not socialising. It's very good, I am happy."

Despite his successes and the life and community he has built for himself in the UK, Seyfu is still waiting to hear his fate from the Home Office. Unsure if he could be forced back to a country that is unsafe for him, he struggles to sleep and often finds it difficult to eat. This situation has greatly affected his wellbeing and he feels that it has a dramatic effect on his running.

The team of coaches at The Running Charity continue to work with Seyfu around his immigration status and emotional wellbeing, ensuring that his voice continues to be heard. Seyfu's dream is to be able to stay, to compete and, ultimately, to win for the UK, a country that he calls home.

ENGLAND HAS GIVEN ME SO MUCH, IT'S MY HOME

"I am in the place I need to be. I want to follow my dreams. I want to be an international runner. I love my nation Ethiopia, but I want to run for GB. England has given me so much, it's my home, my country and I want to run for my country."

Seyfu was talking to Alex Eagle of The Running Charity.

BACK ON TRACK
FRANKIE LYNCH

I have always run. I was in the relay and cross-country teams at school. Ran my first marathon when I was 21 years old and ran on and off for the next 20 years doing distances up to half marathons. I didn't think a lot about it, I just did it. I always enjoyed it and managed to stay fit. I promised myself to run the London Marathon by the time I was 50 which I successfully achieved in 4hrs 40mins. I was delighted but knew I wanted to do it again, run it faster, run it better. So, I joined my local running club, Thames Valley Harriers (TVH).

I WANTED TO BE ANONYMOUS, JUST ANOTHER RUNNER

Around about the same time my life changed dramatically. My partner of 24 years was diagnosed with small cell lung cancer and had just started her treatment. As a relatively new member of the running club I didn't know many people which I thought was a blessing – it meant I didn't need to speak to anyone. I didn't want to have to tell my story. I wanted to be anonymous, just another runner there to improve their running. When you are running round a track doing pyramids, reps, sprints etc, thankfully you can't think of anything else. By the end of the evening I would always come away feeling lighter, optimistic about the days ahead and physically tired out which meant I might sleep better, something I had not being doing recently.

I DECIDED TO RUN THE LONDON MARATHON IN MEMORY OF ANN

Two years later I was on my own and a widow at only 53. My life had collapsed, and the love of my life was no longer with me. I decided to run the London Marathon in memory of Ann and fundraise for cancer research. I worked out my training plan and started to run. I ran like I had never run before, not because of the discipline of sticking to my training plan, or the mileage I was clocking up, but because I ran through my grief. The pain, the anger, the hurt, the loss, the loneliness, the injustice, the incomprehension of losing someone so close to you. There were days when I ran with tears streaming down my face; other times when my entire body was too heavy to move and I felt like I was dragging a ton of concrete around with me.

IT TAKES YOU TO ANOTHER PLACE

Running gave me the space and time to work through the emotions that come with grief. It never expects answers or smart solutions, it takes you to another place and brings you out somewhere better than where you started. It provides structure and purpose to your day when all you want to do is stay under the duvet and cry. It gave me a reason to live when I didn't want to be alive. And stay alive I did.

I FELT MY PARTNER WAS WITH ME ALL THE WAY!

I ran the 2016 London Marathon 15 minutes faster than previously. I felt that my partner was with me all the way and at one point when it was particularly tough, she took my hand and dragged me along.

The elation of crossing the finishing line was immense. I was at peace with myself again and my partner was in my soul to never leave me. Running got me through the worst time of my life and helped me get it back on track to face the next day, and the next and the next.

Frankie volunteers with The Running Charity

MO'S 5,000 MILES
RYAN FRIEL

Volunteer, mentor and fundraiser for the The Running Charity, Ryan recounts his experience of meeting Mohammed Gabiyo.

I attended The Running Charity mentor and volunteer training sessions in the summer of 2018. At the beginning of August, I was matched with a young person called Mohammed. We agreed to run the following Sunday. Mo suggested 6am.

We met at East Ham station in London. As I would get used to, Mo was positive, grateful, and energetic. We got to know each other on the way to Wanstead Flats and our first run together. After completing 7km it was clear that Mo could have kept going, despite not running for three years.

THE LONG AND TREACHEROUS 18-MONTH JOURNEY

Hearing Mo's story was incredibly humbling. A refugee from Ethiopia, he made the long and treacherous eighteen-month journey through Sudan and Libya, across the Mediterranean Sea to Italy, through Europe to The Jungle in Calais, and finally to the UK. Placed in a hostel in East Ham Mo is seeking asylum. Meanwhile, he campaigns for equality and justice for the Oromo people in Ethiopia.

During his voyage to the UK Mo travelled across the Sahara Desert, one of the most unforgiving and severe lands in the world. He was forced to work, handcuffed, beaten by bandits, blackmailed by smugglers, went days without food, and survived on minimum amounts of water, sharing it with 60 others packed into the back of a truck.

We agreed to meet again for the TRC Thursday group session. When I showed Mo a picture from the monthly TRC parkrun at Finsbury Park, he pointed to one of the young people in the photo. "Seyfu... Seyfu.. from the Jungle!" Having made similar journeys from Ethiopia they spent three months together in "The Calais Jungle," attempting to cross the British Channel to seek asylum in the UK. It is truly incredible how TRC brought these two young refugees from the other side of the world together.

MO DID HIS FIRST PARKRUN

A couple of weeks later Mo did his first parkrun, at Wanstead Flats. We ran together at a 'pedestrian' pace, Mo finishing just in front in 21:09. In the TRC monthly group parkrun at Highbury Fields a week later, Mo's time was a full 2 minutes 19 seconds quicker, and we had reached his first milestone, receiving matching TRC Asics running shirts.

Over the next few weeks, Mo's times for 5km were regularly around the 18-minute mark, and we felt strong and ready for our next challenge, the Oxford Half Marathon.

The morning of the run saw perfect conditions, chilly with blue skies, and we ran the whole 13.1 miles together. Pushing each other all the way, we sprinted to the finish line, Mo pipping me to the post once

more, but both finishing in 01:27:18. It was a perfect day, an incredible milestone to reach together two months after meeting, and a credit to Mo for his commitment, work ethic and positive energy.

ROLE MODEL AND MENTOR

Mo officially graduated the TRC mentor programme at the start of November. With his graduation comes the responsibility of being a role model and mentor for his TRC peers. The TRC program was a pleasure to take part in, very well organised and structured, with help from the TRC staff whenever required. It has been a perfect example of how TRC can improve confidence, provide a strong support network, and improve health, both physically and mentally for a vulnerable refugee who travelled 5,000 miles to escape violence and discrimination.

We continue to meet up for a tea and a cookie at KFC and regularly attend the Wanstead Flats parkrun. Mo has had such a positive impact on my life. He is brave, kind, funny and passionate, and it has been a pleasure spending time with him. Without doubt he will be a friend for life, and it was amazing to be part of Mighty Mo's story.

THE MORE I RAN THE FITTER AND HAPPIER I GOT
LISA BUTLER

I hesitated about sharing my story publicly. I know it will make me feel vulnerable and embarrassed, but I am stronger now.

A couple of weeks ago, I couldn't sleep. Nights are the worst time when the paranoia and anxiety step in. So instead of letting the black dog in I sat and wrote these words of self-love and tried to reason why I'm such a mess.

Anxiety kicked in around my fortieth birthday as I reminisced looking at old photos with my mom. One photo stood out. I look happy, beautiful, and carefree. Sweet fourteen with the whole world at my feet. Instead, my life was a nightmare.

At this time, I was a victim of domestic abuse from my 19-year-old boyfriend. No one knew but me. No 14-year-old should suffer the abuse I did. Bruises and wounds heal, scars fade, but the emotional abuse, that never goes away. "You're fat, you're ugly, you're useless, no one loves you, no one wants you" is etched in my brain and won't go away.

Since then I have suffered with my mental health, suicide attempts and many thoughts of repeating. I struggle to accept these feelings and I can't understand why it still bothers me. I'm married to an amazing man, have an amazing family and job, but mental health is difficult to understand. The black dog can reappear at any time.

Three years ago, for no reason at all I was in the black, dark place again. I was particularly upset at my graduation. I had excelled in two degrees in nursing and midwifery, but I couldn't be proud. I was fat, ugly, everything that had been etched on my brain since I was a teenager. I knew I was on a downward spiral of feeling alone and useless. I didn't want to get treatment, I'm sick of pills, sick of being judged, of being told to pull yourself together. I had to do something and the only person that could help me was me. So, after watching a programme by Katie Hopkins who said you just need to eat less and move more, I decided to try running.

I WENT FROM COUCH TO MARATHON IN A YEAR

Well, I wouldn't really call it running. As a size 24 it was more of a wobble. But I continued, ignoring all the comments and sneers. I ran and the more I ran, the fitter and happier I got. I changed as a person. I started to smile and enjoyed the freedom running gave me. As my body shape changed and my fitness improved so did my confidence. I went from couch to marathon in a year. I went from a size 24 to a 14/16. But the biggest most positive change is my Wallace and Gromit smile. It's real now.

Running has given me a purpose, a release, a way to deal with my mental health. It has brought amazing people into my life, girls I now class as my true friends, in fact sisters. I can tell these girls anything and they know when I'm struggling. They give

me a kick up the arse when needed and vice versa.

I run to improve my physical and mental health, and to be a role model for my daughter. I am her biggest influence and I want her to know that the only person she needs to improve in life is herself.

I'm hoping that my positivity continues. I know I will have blips, but with my friends, family and running I can achieve anything.

BRAVE, BEAUTIFUL AND BOLD WHEN RUNNING

After I was told I was too fat to run a marathon I set up a Facebook group called This Body Runs. I wanted to prove to others that size has nothing to do with running and I want to inspire others to run regardless of their size. The group is going from strength to strength. I have released my own brand of running leggings for all sizes to be brave, beautiful and bold when running.

I EMBRACED THE RUNNING COMMUNITY

For anyone out there in a similar position, speak out, be strong and remember you are loved by who you need to be loved by. Not everyone will like you and that's OK. I'm so glad I embraced the running community.

RUNNING THROUGH CANCER
ANNE BROMLEY

I had been running with my brilliant club, Heathfield Road Runners, since we moved from Northumberland to East Sussex. I ran some races including the East Sussex Sunday Cross Country League and other local 10ks but nothing as serious as a half marathon. My husband Ian and some members of the club were running the Hastings Half Marathon, so I thought why not. I felt the fittest I had ever been, so it seemed like a great opportunity.

March 22nd 2015 came, and I completed the Half Marathon in 1:43. I was amazed that I managed to do that speed, and I still am. I was so chuffed, and I continue to be very proud of what I achieved. I came over the finish line with a dear friend Will, who together with his wife Fleur has provided such amazing encouragement and support to us both. The running club was a great way to be part of our local community, especially when we were new to the area.

I CONTINUED TO RUN UP UNTIL MY FIRST SURGERY

A week after the half marathon I was sitting in a consulting room being given a breast cancer diagnosis at the age of 33. How could I go from being so fit and healthy to needing surgery and chemotherapy in a week? It seemed so surreal. I continued to run up until my first surgery and this gave me space and normality that I really needed.

I went for my first run four weeks after surgery and it was amazing the feeling of air on my face, the freedom, the absolute joy at being able to do it was fantastic. It was giving me back a sense of who I was, not just the cancer patient, I was Anne who loves exercise and wants to be fit, healthy and active. After the initial two miles that first day I continued running, going out when I could with the club and on my own to pass the lonely days off work, with only my thoughts for company and the hospital appointments to fill my day.

RUNNING KEPT ME HEALTHY AND STRONG, AND HELPED MY BODY COPE

Chemotherapy began once I had healed from the surgery, and I continued to run. I truly believe that running kept me healthy and strong, and helped my body cope with the strain that chemotherapy put on it. I managed to continue to run during three of my six cycles of chemo, completing a 10 km race on my birthday, the day before my third chemo, with my sister watching on. This was so special and kept me going. I continued running when I could, until it was no longer possible due to the side effects causing too much pain and fatigue.

Thanks to my running club and the community of runners I have around me, my husband and my family who supported me throughout and continue to do so, I have been able to get back to running, not to the speed I was doing, but that's OK. I relish the enjoyment and freedom

running gives and I have since been able to run a couple of marathons.

SIMPLY BEING OUT IN THE FRESH AIR AND ALIVE

Running is special for so many reasons, all of which are so personal to each of us.

For me running through our beautiful countryside, not for speed, distance, or records, but for the enjoyment of simply being out in the fresh air and alive is what keeps me going.

RUNNING
JOURNEYS

I CANNOT IMAGINE MY LIFE WITHOUT RUNNING

CELESTINE AGBO

As a child I ran for my life, now I run for joy. I've no idea why I'm so good at it but could probably connect my earliest memories of running to when I lived in a village in Nigeria, before the Biafran War arrived when I was seven and devastated everyone's lives.

With over 30 Marathons, including about 20 consecutive London, I could not have had a better ending than in 1999 when I assisted an audacious MS sufferer to achieve one of her life's ambitions by taking part in the marathon. We started at the very back and almost an hour later we cleared the starting line with her walking frame and me by her side. It was challenging to keep up the positive outlook of the day when the refuse collectors had also passed us. To this day I'm delighted to say that was the last person to finish the 1999 London Marathon. The next morning at 2.30 am, we had to write in for our T shirts and medals because all the marshals had gone. So we had no official finishing photograph either. Even the Queen had turned her lights out for the night by then.

In 1995 I thought I'd do something different, so I became the first person to run the entire London Marathon backwards, yes backwards, looking over my shoulders unaware that I'd set a record that lasted over 15 years. Not having much interest in the competitive aspect of beating a previous time, I realised that could actually make more money for charity by being a 'fun runner', a term I actually do not like, simply because

marathon running hurts and wasn't really that much fun for most of the duration, hence fancy dress.

I RAN IN MY WIFE'S SARI ONE YEAR

I ran in my wife's sari one year, bejewelled and with full make up. The gold clip-on earrings turned more heads than my lipstick. A year later when I managed a father's support service I ran with a child in a sling, simply to illustrate the love and bonding between fathers and their child. I should stress that it wasn't a real child.

Here's a funny bit: one year during the marathon I could hear "Come on black man!" Three miles, five miles, the chants persisted as I ran on thinking "Why was the crowd shouting for me that way?" At the seventh mile I turned and realised that the crowd was actually cheering "Come on Batman."

Although I do not run that often I cannot imagine my life without running. Running continues to be one of the most effortless things I do. I love the feeling I get from it. For me it is the best therapeutic thing I do for myself and for my wellbeing. As the child in an Ibo village, who loved to dance naked in the downpour, I've continued to honour the rain as my best running condition, and no matter where I am or what I'm doing if the rain arrives I simply have to be in it, preferably running.

I AM A RUNNER
MEL HEALE

Hi – my name's Mel, and I'm a runner. It still surprises me sometimes that I can introduce myself that way!

Back in 2018 I was signed off work for a few weeks with severe anxiety. I got myself stuck in a vicious circle of comfort-eating, feeling bad about myself, not wanting to – and not feeling able to – leave the house, and turning to food for comfort once again. As my prescribed medication began to take effect and I started to feel a little better in myself, I realised I had to look after my body and mind rather better than I had been doing. I'd heard about the Couch to 5K programme, and although 5K seemed like a distant dream at that point, I was ready to get myself off the couch and to venture out of the door.

MY HUSBAND FINALLY FOUND OUT I WAS DOING IT

At first, I didn't tell anyone I was doing it, keeping it a secret even from my own family. I really wasn't sure whether I'd stick at it and I didn't want anyone to know about it if I 'failed'. It wasn't easy, that's for sure, but it was manageable, and I loved seeing the progress I was making. It also did me a lot of good to be outside in the fresh air, appreciating the nature around me, and giving my thoughts a positive focus to replace the paralysis of anxiety. It was at the end of Week 5 that my husband finally found out I was doing it, and by then I knew I'd complete the programme – partly because I'm a completer-finisher type and was determined to see it through, but partly, to my own astonishment and his, I was actually enjoying running!

WITH ALL BEING MADE SO WELCOME

It felt great to reach the end of the nine weeks and look back to my starting point. By now I'd returned to work but was still fitting in my regular runs, and running was becoming part of my routine and a very important element in managing my anxiety. I invested in some decent running shoes, bought some proper running tops and leggings, and ventured along to my local parkrun. I'd heard of parkrun before and knew a few people who did it and loved it, but I'd wanted to complete Couch to 5K first, so I knew I'd be able to run the whole distance. (I now know that this isn't necessary and walking some or all the way is perfectly fine.) I absolutely loved the whole experience: the enthusiastic encouragement from the marshals; the wide range of speed, experience and age, with all being made so welcome; the automatic PB I achieved, with it being my first one. I was an immediate convert.

Since then parkrun has become part of my Saturday and there needs to be a good reason for me to miss it. It's been great to see my PB gradually come down, I've enjoyed visiting other locations when possible – especially to meet up with friends, and I've also discovered the joy of volunteering and giving something back to the running community.

This community is such a big part of my love for running. Through Twitter I've discovered many like-minded folk, found support, encouragement and advice, and been inspired over and over again by seeing fellow runners' tweets. The jubilant triumphs are always great to celebrate, but just as inspiring are the honest confessions of struggles. I've made some great connections and very real friendships this way. It's been a joy to meet up with so many of my Twitter friends at parkruns, races and events, and I look forward to more opportunities to add to my collection of 'Melfies'!

I RUN FOR MEDALS. I RUN FOR FUN.

So now, just over two years on, I know I 'am' a runner. I run to improve my fitness. I run to help manage my mental health. I run to challenge myself. I run to give myself headspace. I run for the joy of it. I run for medals. I run for fun. I run in the sunshine, the rain, the wind, the snow. I run with friends. I run alone. I run as part of the running community.

I am a runner.

I run.

PROMISES, PROMISES
SUE RESSEL

"Promise me you won't let me run another?"

"I promise" my husband said as he helped me hobble to the tube after my first marathon.

It had all seemed so simple six months earlier when I decided to run a marathon for my 50th birthday. You see, my twin had run 13 marathons in his 20s. I'd run zero. Sure, I'd run track in college for four years, but my cross country career started with the season opener jog of 12 miles and ended with the same run, a dark blue toenail (you know what that means), and my vow to never run more than five miles – ever. Three children, jobs, housework, all meant I'd run 10 times in 10 years.

So, what happened? I overheard someone say, "I'd like to be able to tell my grandchildren that I did X." No memory of what their 'X' was, but it got me thinking what mine would be. Something physical. "Sky dive?" Be serious. "Climb Everest?" No way. "Run a marathon?" That seemed possible. And what was more intriguing is that it would require me to work smart, not just hard. You cannot possibly train for a marathon in six months unless you know what you are doing. That appealed, so a Google search later, and I was off and running. Literally.

"Don't increase distances more than 10% a week." I may be no good at math, but even I know that a 10% increase on zero is still zero. Still, a gentle totter turned into a 20 min jog turned into a five-mile slog, and before I knew it, the miles were adding up.

Running as you get older teaches you so much. That something will always hurt, but you can work through it. That getting out in the rain is actually enjoyable. That vanity is a waste and camaraderie is everything. Running when we travelled showed me places usually inaccessible to tourists. Most remarkable was that the more I ran, the younger I became. That's not just smart, that's magic. I was hooked.

Race day arrived with sun and crowds. There is no feeling on earth to match running alongside 60,000 other people while thousands more cheer you on. Finishing brings tears of joy and pain.

So, my husband knew exactly what would happen when I hobbled up to collapse in his arms.

"Promise me you won't' let me run another?" I groaned.

"I promise" he said.

The full sentence he was thinking?

"I promise to be there next year to catch you at the finish line."

And he was.

THE NINJUTSU RUNNER
JOE OGBONNA

"With me now Joe" my martial arts teacher said, showing me how. "Do one press-up, one squat-thrust, one squat."

"Good. Now, two of each." "You got it, Joe. Now continue like so until you get to ten," he said as he walked away to teach the rest of the class.

The he turned back after a few steps "Oh, when you get to ten, work your way back to one of each. Go on, my son!"

I was worried, and thought, "What have I got myself into here? All I wanted to do was run."

I SOUGHT TO SCARE MYSELF INTO RUNNING REGULARLY

Not run away, although I was tempted when I could no longer keep track of counting press ups, squat thrusts, and squats. I mean, I already enjoyed running, but was just frustrated at my inconsistency at it, and in my warped thinking I sought to scare myself into running regularly, by proving to myself that I was unfit.

Logical and strategic, isn't it? So, twenty years ago in May, I turned up for that ninjutsu class, to scare myself.

You know what? It worked.

I have run the London Marathon twice, run the 10 mile Cabbage Patch most years for the past 10 years, and run just under 10 km every Sunday morning. The running also helps me progress in my martial arts.

THE FIRST TIME
ADRIAN KERR

It was in 2000 and something, back when you could still smoke in the pubs. I had left my job in London and returned to full-time education and was supping a pint with my new Uni friends in Sheffield.

Listening to them talk about running cross country, I picked up my Marlboros and lit up, content in the knowledge that I would be sleeping in late, staying warm, starting my weekend as I always had.

WE'RE DOING A WARM UP RUN TOMORROW MORNING, WHY DON'T YOU JOIN US?

Drifting off into my thoughts of how I was going to spend the weekend, JC (aka Dave) looked across the table and said "We're doing a warm up run tomorrow morning, why don't you join us? But first you have to put that cigarette out!" I don't know what it was that made me say yes. Was it the beers, the genuine interest to see what this running malarkey was about, or something deeper? Whatever it was, in that moment I was determined to make a change, but first I would finish my beer and crisps.

It was a cold and crisp morning. I had dragged myself out of bed and I was set, ready to go, dressed in an old cotton T shirt, shorts, and a pair of what is best described as pub trainers. I listened to JC outline the route as I drank my coffee and ate my bacon butty to help with the hangover. I heard him say "We set off together, turn right up the hill and…" my head was spinning. I thought I would just keep them in sight and remember to turn right.

JUST ONE STEP AT A TIME

Bundling out of the front door of the house, the cold air hit my face, I felt winded, as my eyes watered. I couldn't see the guys, or ahead of me, as I was looking down at the ground finding my feet and adjusting to this alien landscape. Within what felt like seconds I had lost sight of the group but was still confident I could just turn right and then make some sort of loop back to base, just one step at a time (which has since become my running mantra).

Heart pounding, lungs filling with mucus and cigarette tar, I was building momentum as I approached the turning into Bolehill Lane. Looking up I came face to face with what seemed to be the Eiger itself. No sign of the guys. I was wet from the sweat, red faced, blowing, and gasping for air but I had come this far – about 200m – and would conquer this mountain or die trying.

Reaching the summit, I stopped out of necessity. Looking around waiting for my vision to return I saw the morning view come into sharp focus, like seeing the world for the first time. I looked down the road I had travelled and turned to see the road ahead. I had a choice, to walk back to the house with my excuses already

forming in my mind, (I didn't have the right trainers or kit etc) or push on, a chance to do something I had never managed before. So, I turned to follow the rising sun.

Eventually I made it back to the house, worn out, every limb aching and looking like I had been put through the washing machine. But I was glowing, full of accomplishment and proud to be still standing. The guys had completed their warm up run and left the house to go to their cross country race. Standing alone in the kitchen with a hot mug of tea I knew if I could achieve this, I could achieve anything, just one step at a time.

I HAD STARTED MY RUNNING JOURNEY

Later that weekend we worked out I had run a little over my first mile in the wrong direction. But was it? I had started my running journey.

The lads bought me my first running watch from the market with just a basic start/stop, no GPS, which I still have to this day.

Eighteen years later, after many miles, a few cheeky beers along the way, and lots of laughter with lifelong running friends, I find myself chasing new running goals. Still taking it one step at a time.

BEST RUN ON THE PLANET
JOE SMITH

Sausalito is a little tourist town on the north side of the Golden Gate Bridge across the bay from San Francisco. It's a magical place with a rich musical history. Otis Redding wrote the famous 'Sittin' On the Dock of the Bay' here in 1968, and Sly and the Family Stone, Fleetwood Mac and Stevie Wonder all recorded albums here.

I love to run. Since moving to Sausalito, a challenging route that I try to do once every couple of weeks is a 10km trail run that takes in the Bay, the Golden Gate Bridge, and the stunning Marin Headlands.

OTIS REDDING BLARING IN MY HEADPHONES

With Otis Redding blaring in my headphones, I leave my house running downhill to Second Street where I have to take on one of several challenging climbs. If you've ever tried to cycle from Sausalito to San Francisco, a favourite ride by many San Franciscans, you'll know what I'm talking about.

As you climb out of Sausalito you take a left off the main street on a road that hugs the shoreline of Richardson Bay down towards Fort Baker. This is a beautiful spot where I have seen deer on the roads and dolphins on the water.

Meandering down to Fort Baker is a welcome respite on the legs after the initial climb out of Sausalito, and as you turn right downhill towards a huge American flag that sits in the middle of Fort Baker,

the breeze from the Bay gives you an added boost.

BUT THE CLIMBING HAS JUST BEGUN

Past Fort Baker, and what must be one of the most beautiful settings for a coast guard base, you hit the Golden Gate Bridge. With its huge red girders above you, the biggest climb of the run begins. The road switches back as you climb and after several agonising minutes you are at the

entrance to the north side of the bridge, but the climbing has just begun.

ABOVE THE GOLDEN GATE BRIDGE THE VIEW IS WORTH THE BURN IN YOUR LEGS

From here you take a left onto the SCA trail in the Marin Headlands National Park. The climb continues over rocks and wooden bridges, but as you climb high above the Golden Gate Bridge the view is worth the burn in your legs.

As you continue on the SCA trail the bay is on your right and the Pacific Ocean comes into view on your left. The final ascent is the peak of the SCA trail where you get a 360 degree view of Sausalito and the entire San Francisco Bay. I normally catch my breath here. The climb is around 1,000ft so you really have to earn this view, but it's stunning.

From here the trail takes you back home towards Sausalito via the Alta trail. Legs are jelly, but there can't be many better runs on the planet.

RUNNING WITH DIABETES
TOM BARTLETT

It is not because I am diabetic that I run. I run because it makes me feel healthier. I run so I can have guilt-free chocolate and cake. I run because of the endorphin-induced mood boost after a good session. I run because of the window of time that it gives you to think about things. I run because it is an embodied activity, so different to that of sitting at a desk. I love feeling more a part of the physical world, as my body works to transport me through it. And I run because in this seemingly fractured and often confusing world, fraught with difficulties and challenges, setting yourself a running goal is a satisfying way of achieving something real.

Being diabetic is an extra layer of challenge on top of the other things that go into the recipe for good running – the type and amount of training, nutrition, kit, psychology, etc. To run successfully I need to manage my blood sugar, which isn't always easy; however, it can be done. Given the numerous health benefits of exercise, running is recommended for diabetics just like it is for non-diabetics.

As a diabetic I have an involved relationship with carbohydrates, which are one part of the nutrition picture. Carbohydrates are absorbed into the blood as sugar. As a type 1 diabetic, I produce no insulin, so I have a pump that infuses it into me. In simple terms, insulin acts to remove sugar from the blood and store it for future use. If you're trying to run, that is not what you need. So, the crucial test for a diabetic is balancing carbohydrate intake with insulin intake. Sounds simple... but difficulties arise because neither insulin nor carbohydrate uptake are instantaneous. The normal rule of thumb is that insulin acts over a four hour period. So, I will have 'insulin on board' for four hours after taking any. I don't want to run with any significant insulin on board because that means my body will be trying to store sugars instead of allowing them to be used to fuel my run. To complicate things further, sensitivity to insulin can increase significantly when doing hard exercise, so the effect of any insulin on board can be magnified. Therefore, adjustments in my diabetic regime are needed if I am going to run.

The runner's experience of managing diabetes varies considerably between individuals. Diabetics new to running should proceed gently, and due consideration must be given to doctors' advice. Bit by bit you will work out how you can manage the condition and enjoy the wonderful benefits of running. I cannot claim to have achieved any records, but I am pleased to have completed four marathons and various other half marathons and races.

Before I ever ran, I doubted whether it could be possible with diabetes. The process of finding out how I could achieve these things and slowly building up to them represents a real personal growth for me. I would recommend running to anyone. Indeed, perhaps diabetics have even more to gain than non-diabetics.

Photo courtesy www.marathon-photos.com

STRETCHING
PETER STAFFORD-BOW

I recall the exact moment I realised I ought to do some exercise. I was perusing my body in the mirror and it struck me that my torso was more reminiscent of a middle-aged man's than of the young, twenty-something buck I was. A washed-up, middle-aged man at that, with ungrateful teenage children and a wife long departed for a more aerobic relationship with her Pilates coach. I inspected my reflection. Perky breasts that wouldn't have disgraced a renaissance cherub. Side handles like an over-upholstered Ottoman. And a stomach that had more in common with a three litre wine pouch than a steely six-pack. More manatee than man, frankly. Exercise was required, no doubt about it. But I didn't fancy being flung around by a black-belted sadist, the local gym was infested by steroid-addled psychopaths, and I was allergic to the type of person that enjoys ball games. The only option was running.

I FOUND THE MILD SORENESS IN MY LUNGS BUILDING INTO A RATHER UNPLEASANT BURN

I pulled on my knackered school trainers and began a confident trot along the optimistically named Parkland Walk, an abandoned railway line connecting Finsbury Park with Highgate Station. Other than a slight wobbling sensation, as though my torso had been replaced by a half-full barrel of water, all seemed in order. Soon, however, the track steepened, and I found the mild soreness in my lungs building into a rather unpleasant burn. More dismayingly, the ring of fat surrounding my midriff was now throbbing, very painfully, in time with the slap of my feet against the earth.

MY KNEES SCREAMED, MY CHEST RASPED LIKE A CARPENTER'S PLANE

As rivulets of sweat cascaded down my face, washing salt into my eyes and attracting a cloud of mocking invertebrates, I slowed to a complete halt. I turned and considered the route back home. Downhill seemed a safer challenge, so I broke back into a run, stumbling over tree roots and gasping like a pensioner summiting Kilimanjaro. My knees screamed, my chest rasped like a carpenter's plane and my internal organs moaned as they were flung against one another. Somehow, I made it home, climbed the stairs and collapsed on my sofa.

MY SPINE HAD FUSED INTO A SINGLE INFLAMED BONE

When I awoke, all was dark. I attempted to sit up, but my legs appeared to have been lashed to an invisible plank of wood, while my spine had fused into a single inflamed bone, incapable of any

movement without excruciating pain. I spent half the night attempting to claw my way to my bedroom, whimpering and trailing my useless limbs behind me, before surrendering to certain death and passing out.

AS THE WEEKS PASSED, THE FRENZIED GASPING RECEDED

The moral of the story, of course, as a variety of clever clogs informed me the following day, is that one must always stretch after exercise. Despite that initial fiasco, the following week I repeated my run, this time completing it non-stop. As the weeks passed, the frenzied gasping receded, and my enjoyment of running increased. I lost the pounds and my body morphed into a physique that would have had the Ancient Greeks panting with artistic delight. I was a runner. And yes, dear reader, never again did I neglect to stretch after exercise.

Peter Stafford-Bow is the pseudonym of an author writing humorous novels about the wine business.

RUNNING IS MAGIC
SID WILLS

In 1954 when I was 14 Roger Bannister broke four minutes for the mile at the Iffley Road track in Oxford. Friends and I celebrated by running around and around the block of streets in Heaton, Newcastle where I lived. I was so inspired I joined Gosforth Harriers as a junior. I was a daily runner, I ran home and back to school every lunchtime, about a mile each way. I remember aged 11 running through muddy woods to the sea on the Isle of Wight, around a small loch near Pitlochry, also Loch Earn, all at Boy Scout camps.

I left school at 15 and became an apprentice printing compositor. I suddenly found myself working with the secretary of Elswick Harriers, Davy Yule, who became my mentor in many ways. The works manager was involved with Heaton Harriers. He often asked why I was not in his club? My mother said it would be more advantageous for me in Gosforth, as it was a more middle class area.

Sid Wills is centre presenting Serpentine Club awards

THE DAYS OF PLIMSOLLS

I ran cross country, track, and field. It was the days of plimsolls.

At the age of 26 I drew out some money from a Post Office savings account and the drinks were on me. I had decided to leave Newcastle. My next stop was Iffley Road, Oxford, overlooking that famous track. I began working at the Oxford University Press as a compositor/reader. Thirty years or more were to pass before I ran again.

Now 58, I was living in Islington, London.

I had a mini stroke and after a year of feeling quite low, on holiday in Lyon, I remember seeing many people running. I decided, on return to London, to run again. I bought a pair of running shoes, no longer plimsolls. I was working at a special school on Broadwater Farm and began running with two colleagues at lunchtime.

I decided I would like to join a running club. One of my colleagues at the NSPCC where I worked on the phone lines in the evening ran for Thames Valley Harriers. He suggested Serpentine Running Club,

as it was a good central spot, with a lot of mixed ability. Even so I was very nervous about joining.

Being a member of the club (and the club's reputation) has given me wonderful opportunities to get involved in work with the media. My trademark "Running is Magic" first went public when I used it on a BBC programme on speed, jet planes, speed boats and sportspeople. Later I appeared with Gloria Hunniford on her programme, looking at age and running, where she referred to me as Mr Magic.

One of my strong interests has been using counselling skills in running coaching, with new-ish or nervous runners. People would say I take an unorthodox approach, especially after one of my 'off piste' runs which might involve going into a hotel, an art gallery or even a restaurant kitchen. I think I am passing on the magic. With beginners I love using visualisation to make the runs more creative. I often quote The Zen of Running, "If not fun, better left undone."

ONLY I KNEW HOW FAR I'D COME
TOM ALBRIGHTON

When I was young, running meant freedom. Running was hurtling across a playing field, whichever way you felt. Running was intersecting vectors of play, the vapour trails left by the spitfires and superheroes we became at playtime. Later, at senior school, running came to mean the opposite. It was a prison, a torment. The start of every school year was marked by a cross-country run in the local park. It wasn't supposed to be a race – but that's just what you told yourself when you'd finished last. Steve Jackson, who was already six foot, invariably cruised home first, leaving the rest of us labouring up the hill in his wake.

Later still, as an adult, I got fat and unhealthy. I didn't like my body, so I ignored it, and it repaid me by becoming even less likeable. What goes around comes around – and I became round.

OBVIOUSLY, I COULDN'T LET ANYONE SEE ME DOING IT

Eventually, something clicked. I had to take some exercise. Obviously, I couldn't let anyone see me doing it, so I worked through a set of exercises from a book. Counting out 100 high-knee jogs on the spot in my bedroom, I felt something that I hadn't felt for many years. You know that feeling well. It's the one you only get after a run.

Emboldened, I ventured out on to the pavements. It wasn't so bad. Someone beeped their horn at me derisively, but I turned the other cheek. Hey, at least I'm on the right track, I thought. (Now, when I see novice runners out and about, I try to telepathically convey the same sentiment. You go girl. Keep at it mate. You're doing great.) I got home feeling exhausted but exhilarated. Running was a drug – and I wanted another hit.

I HAD TO AWKWARDLY ROTATE MY ENTIRE BODY

Next day I could barely walk. My quads were burning embers, my hamstrings two red-hot steel rods. To get downstairs, I had to awkwardly rotate my entire body, looking like a statue trying to descend a cliff path. I'd learned an important lesson – stretch before and after.

Undaunted, I started running once or twice a week. I liked running to music, and still do – but all I had back then was a MiniDisc player. In terms of reliability and convenience, it was scarcely better than pushing a record player around on a trolley. The iPod Shuffle, when it came, was life changing.

My runs steadily lengthened. Every so often, I added in another segment of ring road, another block of houses. I was doing three miles, then five. I discovered that I could run in the dark, in the rain, even in the snow. Anything but icy pavements, I could deal with.

Soon I was tracking runs on my phone. The data didn't lie and was often weirdly

enough beans. No alcohol and a sound sleep the night before. A positive, can-do mood in the morning. During the run, I needed certain songs, which I duly curated into a '10k quick' playlist. Oh, and no obstructions when crossing the road.

Eventually, I got there: 44:13. Six consecutive miles, each in less than eight minutes. Even a few years before, I'd have thought that was impossible.

But even as I celebrated, I think I knew I'd never do it again. My age, like my 10k time, seemed stuck in the high 40s, with little chance of going much lower. But I'd done it, and that was what really mattered.

MAYBE WHAT REALLY MATTERED WERE THE MANY HILLS I'D CLIMBED

Or maybe it wasn't. Maybe what really mattered were the many hills I'd climbed between my teenage years and now. Not the quick sprint, but the long distance.

Now, I've started running when we visit my parents. I run my old walk to school, the bus route to the pub, the route my dad took to the garage. On my headphones are the songs we loved back then. It's glorious. I ran the school cross country course again. Once, it had been a place of dread and anguish. Now, just a park with some ducks – nothing special. I cruised up the final hill, barely breaking a sweat, but nobody cared. Only I knew how far I'd come.

at odds with how I'd felt during the run.

Talking of PBs, I read that many amateur runners aimed for a sub-45 10k. Could I do that? I tweaked my route to be bang on the distance, and reasonably free of hills. At first I was always 50+. Then high 40s. For several agonising runs, it was consistently 45 something.

To have any chance of making it, I needed all my ducks in a row. That meant just one attempt per week, or I wouldn't have

CONNECTED WITH THE GROUND
HELEN HALL

Pain instigated my journey towards efficient running. Shin splints and sciatica. The 3 S's. The bane of my life because, either together or alone, they made a misery of the one constant that had kept me sane since I was at grammar school – running. I entered the inaugural Stratford-upon-Avon Half Marathon aged 17. I arrived at the event having trained for the full distance, but with two months to go before my 18th birthday, they wouldn't allow me to run it.

I can't remember when the pain started. Running miles in British service-issue DMS boots with packs on backs and pine poles on shoulders during RAF officer training probably contributed heavily to the 'why' in my pain history, but that was long before the 'when'.

I followed instructions, did the exercises, wore uncomfortable insoles, picked up pencils with my toes, sat cross-legged on the floor, and slept on strange shaped pillows. I sat in special seats and dutifully 'rested', not doing the very thing that I loved – I mean, what kind of a solution is that? I tried them all. Some helped a little; some didn't at all; the pain was always there – the only variance was the degree.

Then, in 2002, a breakthrough. The most unlikely predecessor to a barefoot shoe you could imagine, the original and enormous soled MBT trainer, with the ground far, far away from the actual sole of my foot. You may remember them. But the 'B' stands for barefoot, so perhaps it was a clairvoyant peep into the future? Whatever it was, after 21 years of constant sciatic feedback of the grumbling-through-to-yelling varieties, the pain disappeared. Extraordinary.

RUNNING HAS ALWAYS BEEN MY SANITY

Having said goodbye to my 3 S's, I made steady forward progress. During my divorce, I was told my running symbolised 'running away' from my problems. Even if it did to some degree, within 30 seconds of starting a run, the solution to whatever was bugging me at the time would appear, whether I was looking for answers or not. Running has ALWAYS been my sanity as well as my waistline friend.

The launch of Newtons in 2007/8 heralded the very beginning of mainstream awareness of natural running, minimal footwear, and 'barefooting', and in them, we flew on our first run. I PB'd my five-mile loop by eight minutes!

I TRIED ON HIS VIBRAM FIVEFINGERS

Soon after I met Matt Wallden, the wonderful, inspirational MD of Primal Lifestyle. Wearing my much-loved Feelmax toe socks from Finland, I tried on his Vibram FiveFingers (VFFs). There was something in the air. Pose Method and Chi Running were being discussed, online forums were becoming popular and

for our first run. I still remember it. It was dark, it was somewhere off-road, we got lost in the moment and then actually got lost. We laughed, we felt the cool mud squeeze up and squelch between our toes, our arches were stabbed by cruel stones hidden along the path. We ran further than we'd planned, and even that was further than we ought. All three of us probably had one of the best, most joyful, runs of our lives. We were hooked.

Running form was explored and honed entirely unshod along the five-mile local 'Pednor Loop' country lane. It's amazing what you learn about the mechanics of the human frame in motion when you are totally connected with the ground. Returning from one such session, I was stopped by a lovely older lady with blue hair driving a matching blue Volvo estate. She wound the passenger window down and asked, "Are you... alright?" Confirming that indeed I was, she hesitantly pointed to the apparent loss of my senses... "You seem to have – er – forgotten your shoes, dear."

experiences shared. I'd been barefoot and pregnant in East Africa, only to come home and be totally unable to fit into any 'normal' shoe I'd previously owned. My children's feet were perfect until they went to school in the UK and started wearing 'proper shoes'. There was something about shoes that changed feet, but not enough people were talking about it.

We took the plunge. Wearing our first pair of Vibram FiveFinger KSOs, we headed off

I'M STILL RUNNING, WITH AS LITTLE ON MY FEET AS POSSIBLE

Eight Ironmans and many ultras later – with the ice-melting conversation-opener of being the first 'barefoot' Iron(wo)man in the world – I'm still running, with as little on my feet as possible, and still with curiosity.

ONE PERSON TURNED UP
SARAH PRICE

Twenty-seven years ago, I was overweight and struggling with postnatal depression. To be honest life was a bit of a struggle for me, but it's not really something you want to tell people about for fear of frightening them away.

One day, a lady in the village invited me to join her for a run with some friends from the gym. This filled me with horror but a little voice inside me told me to just do it anyway. I turned up with the wrong shoes and clothes, it was a boiling hot day, and by the end of the two mile run I was a sweaty shattered mess but I had a huge smile on my face at the sense of achievement.

Despite finding it incredibly hard I stuck at it, gradually building up the running, and after 10 months I had lost over two stone and entered my first 10k. My self confidence had grown, and I felt I could call myself a runner. Time flew by and my love for running just grew and grew. I have run many races including an ultra-marathon, but one of my biggest achievements was starting a running club for people in my local area.

Over the years people had approached me and asked why I enjoy running so much. Many of them said they would never be able to run. This spurred me on because I knew that if I could overcome all the difficulties, then anyone could, and I knew they too could enjoy the many physical and mental rewards running brings.

At the first meeting one person turned up! The second was more of a success, ten people turned up, most of them beginners. Slowly, slowly I helped them build up their miles and it was so wonderful to see them grow in confidence. Four years on my running club has grown from strength to strength. We now have many runners, and many followers on Facebook, each with amazing stories to tell about their journey to running and how it has helped them.

THE SUPPORT OF THE CLUB HAS BEEN AMAZING

Of course, life can't always be a bed of roses. A couple of years ago a very good friend of mine was diagnosed with terminal cancer, one of the saddest days of my life. I decided that I wanted to run a marathon for her and raise as much money as I could to help others in her position. My friend saw this as a hugely positive thing to do, and I know that it helped take her mind off the terrible pain she was experiencing. She got totally immersed in the fundraising with me and in turn I got involved with journeys to hospital with her so she could receive treatment. I met some incredibly brave people there, it was a very humbling experience, and in eight weeks we raised over £12,000. Sadly, my friend passed away last October. Once again, my running has seen me through some very difficult times and the support of the club has been amazing.

LIAM, MISHA, PEPSI AND I

CHRISTIAN WOLMAR

There was no sudden epiphany, but at some stage in my mid-fifties I became addicted to running. Not in a bad way. It is well under control. A run two, three, or – in a good period – four times a week means that it does not dominate my life, but is a very important part of it. I would go further. It keeps me fit and feeling far younger than my 71 years would suggest, as on the days I run I have more energy than on those when I opt for a leisurely breakfast.

REWARDED BY A FRY UP IN THE CAFE

I kind of fell into it when I started running with my daughter Misha who was around 15 at the time and it was a way of seeing her as I had just split up with her mother. Our start was modest, perhaps 10 or 15 minutes up and around Parliament Hill on Hampstead Heath and then rewarded by a fry up in the cafe down the bottom.

Christian Wolmar centre

But it soon became more than that. There was a dog involved, too, Pepsi, a Border Collie who was far more excited about the running than either of us. Staying in a house in Umbria on the side of a hill that summer, the three of us started running to the top, a nasty 2km climb that we could not manage at first. And within a couple of weeks, it became easier, and we could go all the way round a circuit of about 10k.

And we had a newcomer, a new friend who has become my regular running partner, Liam, an Irish further education teacher. He only had sandals and could barely manage the first 1km up the hill at first but then by the end of the holiday he was doing the full 10k. I gave him only one word of advice, which I had followed: start off slow. There is nothing worse than running at a full gallop and finding that you can only do a few hundred metres.

Then it became a routine. Liam, Misha, Pepsi, and I became the 'core four'. The dog would corral us, checking on the tail runner and urging them on with little nips and barks. It was by no means always the four of us. Misha went off to university and the dog sadly passed away, while other friends and family sometimes joined in,

ut it became regular. A couple of 5ks in the week, and a 10k at the weekend, nearly always on the Heath. I lost around a stone o be 13 ½, a weight I have kept now for 15 ears and which for a six-footer of medium uild is perfectly OK, even though I could till lose a bit. And the best of it is that I pretty much eat what I want, though am a bit areful about too many buns and biscuits.

iam and I, and occasionally Misha, started ntering races. There were several 10ks nd a few half marathons. The first one, t Southend, nearly killed us, run in 30C heat with insufficient water stations and neither of us knowing quite how far

13.1 miles was. But others were more successful. Liam managed a half marathon in under 2 hours, and I did a 10k in just over 50 minutes. But it was never about that. It was about the regular pounding of the streets and the Heath, the routine of always doing it come rain or shine, the text messages waking each other up, and the joy of feeling good after a nice long run. And don't be fooled. It is a drug. There is nothing better than those endorphins kicking in, the coolness of the sweat all over your body and the pleasure of feeling cleaner than you ever do after the shower. It is a glowing experience.

RUNNING HURTS SOMETIMES
MICHELLE MORTIMER

Age 12, I was volunteered by my class to run the 800m at sports day. I was never an athletic child, and the thought of running around a track, with the entire school watching, filled me with dread. I was so worked up about it, that when I went to the track to have a practice run with two of my friends, I experienced my first ever panic attack. I was thinking about how I would probably come last, and how much it would hurt, and how embarrassing it would be. Those emotions just enveloped me in absolute panic. Tears. Snot. Gasping for air. I never did end up taking part in that race, and I didn't even consider running again until I was in my 20s.

THOSE FIRST TEN MINUTES OR SO AS YOU WARM UP CAN FEEL AWFUL

Now I understand that running does hurt sometimes. Those first ten minutes or so as your body warms up can feel awful, and now I understand the science behind why that happens, I wish that I had understood that as a child. Perhaps I would have given running more of a chance at an earlier age, and perhaps incorporated a warm up before trying to run as fast as I could.

MY SIDE OF THE STORY
NEIL JOHNS

I bought these trainers at Decathlon in 2006 when I split up with my then girlfriend – a typical break-up resolution from a man in early middle age to get fitter, as I remember.

BUT MOSTLY THE TRAINERS SAT IN THE HALLWAY

I did run a bit around Peckham Rye, but mostly the trainers sat in the hallway being gently mocked over the years by my teenage children and their friends, who thought them too uncool, too ugly and, I imagine, simply too 'dad'.

After a few years they started a new life as my gardening shoes, though mostly relaxed in the hallway alongside the children's endless succession of Vans in increasingly large sizes. But then something remarkable happened.

MY SON STARTED TO DEVELOP A LOVE FOR THE SHOES

About two years ago my son started to develop a love for the shoes and, more recently, has taken them running again for the first time in maybe a decade.

I'm not sure the falling-apart soles are up to it, but who am I to say. He's borrowed my shirts and coats from time to time. I suspect they have more fun when they are with him. And so, the story goes on. Oh, and three years ago I got back together with the girlfriend, but that's another story.

RACING TALES

JUST GO A BIT FASTER
ROGER SAWTELL

I am 93 and for 92 of those years I did not show any interest in running. I seemed to prefer swimming or just walking, all over the world. But last October (2019) my always optimistic friend said, "Why not try parkrun, you can always drop out if you feel a heart attack coming on." Ha, blooming ha!

So, on a cold Saturday morning I was surprised to find myself with about 500 other runners on Northampton Racecourse, which in fact is a large park that was once a racecourse. Amazing. I had glucose tablets, but none of the gear which the website recommends. I soon settled at the back end alongside parents with pushchairs and dog walkers, half jogging and half 'power walking', a term I had not heard before. Spontaneously, we were encouraging each other to keep going and there was a wonderful co-operative spirit which I had not anticipated. On the run I made friends with Isaac, aged 9, running with his dad, but stopping now and then to examine an interesting tree or perhaps talk to a dog, so I was just about able to keep up with him. "I'm not 9," said Isaac, "I'm 9¾."

Roger Sawtell is third from right

YOU WERE ALSO FIRST IN YOUR AGE GROUP

Having staggered across the finishing line in about 46 minutes the Race Director said, "Do you want the good news or the bad news?" Okay, give me the bad news. "You were last in your age group."

Oh calamity, why don't I just stay at home and have another cup of coffee for breakfast. "However," he said, "The good news is that you were also first in your age group. We have never before had anyone in the age group 90-94." The first to congratulate me was the redoubtable Bob who has completed 377 parkruns, a wonderful record which I will never equal. But he's a mere 86. We're all in this together. I was hooked.

THESE SOCKS WILL HELP YOU KNOCK SEVERAL SECONDS OFF YOUR PB

Then at Christmas it was decided to do a family run. We have three daughters; the youngest one offered to run with me

at the back of the pack, the eldest co-ordinated the group, the middle one gave me a pair of superior 'running socks.' One sock was marked L and the other marked R. They both looked identical apart from the marking, but I dutifully put the L sock on the left foot and the R on the right, hoping they would live up to the maker's claim – "These socks will help you knock several seconds off your Personal Best (PB)." Hope springs eternal.

ELEVEN OF US GATHERED IN NORTHAMPTON

Anyway, on 28 December, our son ran in Seattle where he lives, and eleven of us gathered in Northampton, three generations and Sunny the dog, who seemed a bit discombobulated with all these people hurrying about. Each of the family group ran at their own pace and after each had registered their time, they jogged back to us tail-enders so that eleven of us eventually crossed the finishing line together, including the dog. Lovely. Youngest grandson was first home in around 25 minutes, and I was last in 44 minutes 50 seconds, by which time many of the other 544 runners would be back home drinking coffee. It must be the socks because this time is my PB and puts me on an age graded score of 74.1% which is Regional Level, better than Local Level. "Just go a bit faster," said the Race Director, "and you will be at National Level for your age group." Not likely.

THE AGONY AND THE ECSTASY
HUGH BALFOUR

"This is how death must feel." From that rather chilling opening line of Richard Askwith's classic book on fell running, Feet in the Clouds, I was hooked. A friend gave it to me at the end of 2005, and fell running sounded like the most bonkers activity you could imagine. I couldn't wait to try it. So, two years later, on a day of low cloud and rain, I lined up at the start of my first real fell race in the small Welsh village of Llanbedr in the Black Mountains.

I had the requisite kit – full waterproof body cover, map, whistle, compass, and emergency food. I knew the race was 17 miles with 5200 feet of ascent and I knew where the 6 checkpoints (CP) were, but I had no idea of the route, and was not helped when the race organiser, John Darby, who was also running, told us not to follow him as he might get lost!

WE WERE IN THICK CLOUD WITH ONLY THE FAINTEST PATH TO FOLLOW

I set off strongly over the first two mountains, Pen Cerrig Calch and Pen Allt-mawr, and joined up with a runner from Tring, Rick Ansell, who clearly knew what he was doing, leading me down a brutal descent, then the equally brutal 1200 foot climb up Pen y Gadair Fawr. At the top we were in thick cloud with only the faintest path to follow. I stuck to Rick like glue, which meant running flat out over what was fortunately an easy mile of descent.

At the bottom we splashed through a stream and while Rick climbed a gate, I thought I would vault the barbed wire fence next to it. When I landed, both calves locked solid with cramp. My scream elicited an enquiry of concern from Rick, but I assured him I was OK. True I wasn't injured, but I thought my race was over. I was in agony and six miles from home. Then I remembered that footballers get cramp and carry on, so after a bit of stretching I set off up the next mountain.

MY QUADS WERE BURNING WITH CRAMP

The next two hours were probably the most painful of my life. As I headed up towards the third checkpoint at the summit of Chwarel y Fan, my quads were burning with cramp, a sensation that really didn't ease much for the rest of the race. Overtaking runners encouraged me as I staggered along, and the weather started to clear up, and the last hour was in glorious sunshine. Then I had a piece of really good luck.

The run from CP 3 to CP 4 on Bal Mawr is an easy, beautiful run along a gentle ridge, followed by a boggy descent from Bal Mawr through a forest to CP5 on the road at Pont Cadwgan. The first trick is to get the right forest – there are three to choose from. My good luck was to be caught up by a woman who knew the way and again, pain notwithstanding, I stuck with her to the road.

IT LOOKS LIKE YOU'VE COME THE SCENIC ROUTE

I was not so fortunate climbing up through the woods to CP 6 on the summit of the final mountain, Crug Mawr. I now know that the best route is to stay in the forest, climbing steeply up a stony narrow path. Instead I headed out onto the open fellside and after blundering through bracken and heather was fortunate to find a path that led me to easier ground below the summit. As I reached the checkpoint the marshal grinned at me, "Looks like you've come the scenic route".

The final descent, a beautiful fast run on grass, was just a painful hobble. But I made it and was surprised to discover that far from being last, I had come 29th out of 51 finishers, and had done it in under 4 hours.

You may be wondering whether I ever did another fell race. The answer is quite a few.

I have done the Black Mountains six times and my PB is exactly 30 minutes quicker than that first race. I learnt how to manage cramp (a bottle of orange juice with a spoonful of salt and Ibuleve gel), how to pace myself better over long races, and how to dig in and push myself when it gets tough.

THERE IS NOTHING MORE EXHILARATING

There is nothing more exhilarating than pitting yourself against the mountains, running fast over rough difficult terrain, and successfully negotiating the bogs, boulder fields, and becks of the British mountains. Above all there is the camaraderie and friendship of fellow nutters, always ready to chat, encourage, and leave you for dead when the opportunity to speed up presents itself.

THE KAZBEGI MARATHON
RAUL KHARBANDA

The Kazbegi Marathon is the only marathon in the Caucasus Mountains. The route takes runners over a tough and beautiful course in the country of Georgia and is named after the nearby 5,000 metre high Mount Kazbegi. The venue for the run is the town of Stepanstminda, which is sandwiched between the disputed area of South Ossetia, and the sensitive regions of Chechnya and Ingushetia.

THE RUN STARTS AT 1,750 METRES AND CLIMBS TO NEAR 3,000 METRES

Over 24 nationalities assembled for the trail marathon. They came from the USA, Germany, and Japan, for the wonderful mountainous scenery. The run itself starts at 1,750 metres and climbs to near 3,000 metres above sea level. For someone training at sea level, this was a difficult adjustment; for any race at altitude it is advisable to come a few days early to adjust.

A GLORIOUS VIEW OF MOUNT KAZBEGI AND THE TOWN BELOW

The first 6km is spent climbing along a steep trail to the Gergeti Church. A glorious view of Mount Kazbegi and the town below is the reward. A sharp descent into the valley of the Terek River follows. This river has played an important role in the history of the region. The Georgian Military Highway follows its route, carving out the only path over the Caucasus. Puskhin and Tolstoy both travelled on this road and wrote about it in their classics. The long valley of the River Terek was unusual for someone like me more used to the throngs of city marathons. Running alone, all I could hear was the peaceful rustle of the river waters, and the sight ahead of wild horses roaming around. It made me want to stop frequently, and just listen, or take a photo.

However, the valley is not uninhabited; the route passes through the villages of Sno and Juta, with ancient defensive towers. As the area is a border region it has probably contributed to the poverty of the area. The marathon plays a part in bringing tourism and the associated employment to the spectacular area – all of the organisers are from the area, or connected to it, and the runners stay in the warmly welcoming B&Bs of the local people.

The community get fully involved. Many of the local children joined the runners for part of the way and there is an 8km run for locals not wanting to do a full marathon. After the marathon, the people will return to their day to day lives, and it is refreshing to see them embrace the event, and the tourists it brings.

BETTER LATE THAN NEVER
JULIA JAMES

I started running in Autumn 1981 the same year as the first London Marathon. That is most probably what inspired me to take my first running steps. I suppose I imagined that one day it would lead me to running London.

I ran the streets of North London in thick sweatpants and a jumper and listened to music on my Sony Walkman cassette. I felt very conspicuous and quite embarrassed. I did a few organised runs in the 80s and was nearly always the last one home. But I carried on because I really enjoyed it. I really had the bug. Over the years I have had injuries, jobs, illnesses, births, and deaths that prevented me from running. I have often heard myself say I will never be able to run again, but at 63 I am still managing to get out there. I'm still at the back, but I'm still running.

I saw family and friends run marathons and I saw how hard it was, and I always said I would never put myself through that. I have cheered and supported so many people running the London Marathon and I can tell you that doing that is extremely hard work!

And then in 2015 I decided it was time to run my first and only marathon. When I was spectating, I saw people older, less fit, and even slower than me. I thought if they can do it why can't I? So, I decided to do it before I turned 60. My mother had died at 60. She had MS. She couldn't walk. It felt important to me to do something because I could. At the same time, I was able to run

in memory of my mother and raise money for an MS charity.

Two thousand and fifteen was Paula Radcliffe's last London Marathon. We had a lot in common. It was also going to be my last marathon. We were both runners; she was fast, and I was slow. We both had goals; she aimed for 2:30, I aimed for 5:00. But as Paula said "I am just grateful that I can run."

But I didn't manage to do the marathon in 2015. About three weeks before the big day with my training plan duly ticked off, I got flu. Real flu that kept me bed-bound and weak for over a month. I had raised a huge amount for charity. I had involved friends and family in my journey and suddenly it was not going to happen. I couldn't imagine having to go through all that training again.

But of course, I did.

In 2016 I did it. I don't even remember what my time was. I really didn't care! I just felt ecstatic to have completed something that I had set out to do. It had taken me 35 years to get there.

ODE TO JOY
PHILIPPA PERRY

Beethoven's 'Ode to Joy' is a lone voice and then gradually other people join that voice and they are of the same mind. Together we are so much more powerful than one person on their own. I find that incredibly moving. I think that's why I used to find running moving. Because I used to run a bit and I always wanted to do the London Marathon – not any other marathon – the London Marathon. And when eventually I managed to do the London Marathon – the joy I felt running all in the same direction with 50,000 people. I think this is what 'Beethoven's Ode to Joy' sums up for me. That feeling of like yeaaaah! – we're in it together – I just love that.

Philippa Perry is a therapist, writer and broadcaster.
Extract from Private Passions, BBC Radio 3.
Photo courtesy Justine Stoddart.

THE JOY I FELT RUNNING ALL IN THE SAME DIRECTION WITH 50,000 PEOPLE

WHAT YOU PUT IN IS WHAT YOU GET OUT

NICK BESTER

In 2016 aged 26, running coach Nick Bester was the youngest of the top 100 finishers in the Comrades Marathon in South Africa, placed 74th overall out of 16,000 starters in a time of 6 hours and 28 minutes.

IT'S A BRUTAL 89KM

The Comrades is a race I have the utmost respect for. It's a brutal 89km ultra marathon. The route from Pietermaritzburg on higher ground to Durban at sea level alternates in direction every year, making the one a down run and the other an up run.

It's a race that is built only for the toughest of the tough and must be completed within 12 hours. About 16,000 people make the start line, around 12,000 finish, of whom 70-80% do so within the last hour. As soon as the clock hits the 12-hour mark, the officials pull a rope across the finish line, stopping every runner who has just missed it. It's heart breaking to see the devastated faces of these exhausted runners who have come so close but will go home without a medal. That pretty much defines the Comrades Marathon: it takes no prisoners.

The training for this race was the hardest part. In running, what you put in is what you get out. There are no shortcuts. for training. The two most important things training for Comrades are: time on the legs getting used to mileage, and doing hilly, undulating runs. I was fortunate enough to live in a hilly area. It wasn't always easy leaving the house at 4.30am in the dark,

half asleep, having to start on an uphill. But it was a hill I'd later thank myself for running up every day. Race day was hard, but if you trained properly, the brutality of the training was harder.

It's important to get good rest the second night before the race, because no one sleeps well knowing you're running Comrades the next day. On race day, I would typically wake up at 3am for a 5.30am start. Then the usual race routine would begin. Like a typical runner, last-minute self-doubt creeps in. Should I have an extra slice of toast? Should I pack extra gels? Should I try go to the bathroom just one more time? It happens to all of us runners: you know your pre-race routine works like it has in the past, but you doubt it every time you have a big race.

When you get into your start pen at around 5am, the true Comrades spirit really kicks in. The anticipation of 16,000 runners on the start line, revving to go, creates a buzz and a vibe which rattles through your bones. You sing the national anthem, followed by a traditional South African song 'Shosholoza', then by the time they start playing 'Chariots of Fire' almost every athlete has a tear in their eye. I very rarely get emotional, but when it comes to the start and finish of Comrades... I cry like a baby. The cock then crows three times, then the gun goes off, and finally you're on your way, knowing the next time your legs stop moving is after a gruelling 89 kms.

Pacing and getting the right nutrition

during this race is more important than anything. Even though I've tried every year, I just can't seem to be able to stomach food during the run. Just about the only thing I could eat were salami sticks, because let's be honest, salami sticks are so yummy.

I usually take five to six gels during the race, and three caffeine shots towards the end. I pre-mix an electrolyte drink that my seconds give me, and have the Energade, Coke and water at the stations en route.

Going out too fast is a crucial mistake made by many. In previous races I have been well behind the field at halfway relative to where I finish. You want to avoid hitting the wall at all costs. My mental preparation for the race is: 30kms warm up, followed by 30kms grinding, followed by 30kms of doing whatever it takes to push as hard as possible until the finish. Usually, I think of someone and dedicate this part to them, which gives me an extra kick and gets me through.

It's the last 30kms of the race that counts.

This is the part where all that training pays off and where the mentally strong come through, the part where the people who went out too fast start paying for it. I sometimes hallucinate at this point. My mind plays tricks on me and my brain goes into survival mode. Once I almost snatched a kid's ice cream from him without thinking. That's the level of exhaustion you're at.

Then finally it is the last kilometre of Comrades. You always finish by doing a lap of a field. The point where your feet touch the grass is the moment you've dreamt of from the start. You know it's just one last lap and you've made it. I've been lucky enough to finish this section with the leading ladies. The crowds go absolutely mental. Finishing with the top ladies also gives you the benefit of some quality TV coverage which my friends and family always appreciate. I could almost hear my Mom screaming at the TV!

Is it possible for me to run a sub six hours one day? Who knows, but I always back myself.

HOW HARD CAN IT BE?
ANDY FOSTER

At 46 years old I was not a runner. In my mind I hated running, I had done it at school and saw no reason to change my mind. However, in 2010 my mum was diagnosed with breast cancer, a mighty big worry for all the family. All we could do was be there and offer support while mum went through the treatment. The relief was immense when she was given the all clear just before Christmas.

Over the Christmas break I got to thinking what I could do to give something back on behalf of my mum. It came to me, "I know" I said "I'll run a half marathon and get sponsored for a breast cancer campaign, how hard can it be?"

I THOUGHT I OUGHT TO DO A BIT OF TRAINING

I thought I ought to do a bit of training so in January 2011 I slipped on some trainers and went to a local lake. I had heard it was a mile around it and thinking I was in reasonable shape my intention was to see how many laps I could do. As I collapsed in a heap gasping for air after only three quarters of a lap, I remember thinking this might be harder than I thought.

While trying to fundraise at work I found colleagues who were runners. They were so helpful and supportive, persuading me to visit a sports shop and buy decent shoes and running gear, and finding me a training program to follow. By April 1 was running about 10k non-stop and beginning to think I might actually do this.

I REFRAINED FROM GETTING CARRIED AWAY AT THE START

Eventually 26th June arrived, and I was lining up at the start with my wife, mum, and dad there to wave me off. I was going to do this, for my mum. It was a gloriously sunny morning, already around 20°C and tipped to get warmer. I heeded the advice of my work colleagues and refrained from getting carried away at the start, although I felt slow as all the seasoned runners disappeared into the distance. It was tough and at about nine miles I slowed to a walk up what the organisers call "Cardiac Hill." There were countless runners resting on the grass verge, taking on water and cooling off. Over the brow approaching mile 10 I heard someone shout "all downhill from here."

I COLLAPSED INTO A CHAIR

They were almost right. With half a mile left to go I felt lifted by the crowds cheering everyone on to the finish line. I found a little extra energy from somewhere and managed a spirited finish, crossing the line after 2hrs 10 minutes, a spent force. I had finished my first ever race and raised about £1,000 for breast cancer. I did it for my mum. They were all waiting for me, and I collapsed into a chair, I didn't care that it was now 32°C.

I ached and hurt for a good few days afterwards, but somehow it felt good. Despite the pain I wanted more. I found

a local running group, The Gentle Joggers, and joined them for their weekly run every Monday. Through them I found Clowne Road Runners and formally joined up. They are such a friendly lot, very encouraging and with a wealth of running experience. Nine years on I am club secretary and have many races under my belt. Who'd have thought it?

LOGISTICAL CHALLENGES

NEIL BRADSHAW

In my first veterans' cross-country race I was a sprightly 50-year-old in the 50 to death age group. I was convinced that with this age advantage I would have a reasonable chance. I was rudely awoken when I looked around after 100 yards to see there was only one limping 70-year-old behind me. At least then I knew where I stood.

I have developed some sort of running sledging style ("you're puffing and blowing a bit there mate – I would ease off a bit") which I know is not really the proper etiquette, but keeps my spirits up.

I HAVE RACED IN DESERTS, CANYONS AND FROZEN ALPS ENJOYING BOTH THE LANDSCAPE AND SOLITUDE

I like races with some sort of logistical challenge. Say a long race where some sort of pacing is important (I subscribe to the give it all you've got and then try to hang on school). My favourites have been some multistage marathons where trying to balance the weight of the food and kit you carry with energy and comfort is always interesting.

I have raced in deserts, canyons and frozen alps enjoying both the landscape and solitude, except a recent experience where a film crew was following the race, constantly asking how we felt. It's difficult to think of anything more interesting when you are tired than "tired".

EATING FOUR LARGEISH SNACKS AND DRINKING FOUR PINTS OF BEER/CIDER

One top logistical challenge has now become my annual A race. "The Great British Beerathon". The format includes running five-ish miles, eating four largeish snacks and drinking four pints of different beer/cider. I am OK at all these disciplines so putting them together means I can normally manage a respectable result (top ten but

yet to podium.) The fun for me is in the preparation, which is slightly different from a normal race. Starting dehydrated and really hungry is a great advantage. Making sure you bring a sensible choice of fancy dress is important – something light and flowing is good. Mexican wrestling masks proved too hot and very inconvenient to drink and eat through. A calm relaxed attitude during the race is recommended as a hurried performance can result in disaster.

I think my future lies in a balance between the more conventional longer races and a few novelty drinking events. I am constantly trying to think of improved strategies for barrel carrying/running/drinking events and dreaming of an unlikely victory.

SIMPLY STAYING ALIVE

My other main strategy is simply staying alive. Watching the field size shrink as you go up the age groups gives me hope for the future.

NO PAIN, NO GAIN
RICHARD PRICE

When I was about seven my dad ran the Scarborough Marathon. I can remember thinking "how can anyone run that far?" and was proud to tell my friends what he had done. It was only when I turned forty that I decided I wanted to have a go at a marathon. I did the Leeds half and felt I was ready for the real thing.

I wanted to run for charity, and in particular the World Cancer Research Fund, as I had family members, friends and clients affected by this terrible illness. When the email arrived in early January confirming that I was in I had 14 weeks to go before the big day. Like any first-time enthusiast I started training with no plan, never hydrated properly, never stretched and thought gels were for elite athletes. Two weeks in I was exhausted, working 12 hours minimum a day, had two young boys, and had to pretend to the wife that I wasn't overtired. She was never keen on me doing the marathon in the first place!

So, I sought professional help and spoke to a running coach who gave me a 12-week plan that was more sustainable than my initial strategy of running as hard, fast, and far as humanly possible every day. The plan was going great and I cut out alcohol (almost totally – two pints a week) and was generally looking after myself. I had one last long run three weeks before the event and was going well, but stopped at 15 miles to get a gel out – I thought if they were good enough for Mo Farah I would give it go!

MY KNEE LOCKED – I WAS IN TOTAL AGONY

To my horror my knee locked. I was in total agony. I tried to start again but the pain was unbearable, so I had to ring my wife Claire to pick me up. I put ice on it and organised a physio who told me to rest and stretch and that it should be OK for the big day.

The week before London I was on holiday with all the family in Cyprus for my father-in-law's 70th. The leg was still not right but the physio felt I would be OK to train when I got there. I did a six-mile run on the first day and felt OK, but by the evening I was in agony and struggling to walk. I started to worry I was not going to be able to do the marathon, and worried about all the sponsorship money raised.

HE ASKED ME IF I WANTED TO DO THE MARATHON

After four days of the holiday the pain seemed to be getting worse, so I headed to the Spa in the hotel to see if there was a physio that could help. The lady on reception said to go to a physio called Carlos who looked after Cypriot international footballers and Olympians. I met Carlos, explained my problem, and he diagnosed it as my IT band. He asked me if I wanted to do the marathon and I said – "more than anything." He said OK, but I had to be prepared for some pain.

I lay on the bed and he got out a metal tool and started rubbing it up and down

The next Sunday was the big day. I had done a four-mile run that week with a bit of pain, but manageable. I had a sleepless night before the race worrying about my injury but wanted to give it my best as I had £10,000 of sponsorship to push me round. The day came, the atmosphere was amazing, and I started off slow as I was determined to finish. My sub four-hour target had gone out of the window. My leg hurt but at mile 15 I knew if I didn't stop I would make it, and then I started to enjoy it. The crowd was electric, and I enjoyed every stride. My mind was in over drive thinking about my Dad in Scarborough all those years ago, the charity I was raising the money for, the people who had been so generous sponsoring me, and the people who had been affected by cancer.

A BIG THANK YOU TO CARLOS FOR THE PAIN

my leg. It was sheer agony and my leg was bleeding due to the pressure. He then started hammering my back and the rest of my body for the remaining hour. At the end he congratulated me on being his only patient not to have sworn or screamed during the first session! He said that the pain may get worse before it gets better and to return twice more before I go home. He was right, I could hardly walk that evening and the next two sessions were just as painful, but I started to feel some movement and less pain on my return home.

I crossed the finish line in 4 hours 20 minutes and was absolutely elated. It was one of my most emotional experiences ever and would urge people no matter how fit, fast, or slow to give it go – sacrifice some time and if you give it your best shot you can do it too. The feeling was amazing, and I loved meeting up with Claire and the boys at the end. Thanks to my Dad for getting me interested in running all those years ago and a big thank you to Carlos for the pain. Without him I would never have been able to do it!

JOY AT THE FINISH
BECCY LOCKSPEISER

I started running in 1983 when my flatmate said, 'Let's run the London Marathon.' I had no idea what that was, but when she explained I thought – yes, let's go for it, why not. So, aged 26, with no previous running experience and smoking 20 fags a day, I started training.

THE SMOKING HAD TO STOP

We'd go for a run and end up in the pub and I would sit there and cough and cough and cough. The smoking had to stop! Running made it easy for me to give up cigarettes as they really don't go together.

SLEEPING OUT ALL NIGHT TO BE ABLE TO RUN 26 MILES

It was only the third year of the event, but it was already very popular and difficult to get into. No one had computers and online entries were a thing of the future. Entries were taken by post on a first come first served basis. However, there was one post box on the corner of Sloane Square which took the first of the entries. So, to guarantee our place, we camped overnight on the pavement along with about a hundred others to get our entries first in the box. The drunken revellers walking past us in the early hours couldn't fathom that we were sleeping out all night to be able to run 26 miles. Times have changed a bit since then.

I THINK THE MARATHON TRAINING PREPARED ME FOR CHILDBIRTH

A short time afterwards I settled down and had a family. I think the marathon training prepared me for childbirth.

The build-up and preparation.

A certain amount of pain.

And a great elation and joy at the finish!

JOE IS STILL FASTER
TOM ANTHONY

At last Joe and I would run a marathon together, in Valencia. First my knee, then his, had denied us when we had planned marathon runs together. We would stay together and complete the course as one.

"Slow-down" Joe coached me, his experience helping me hold back. "Go ahead if you want to Joe" I would offer. We stayed together until mile 16.

WHERE'S JOE?

I felt strong and emotional, thinking of my mother who had died two months earlier. I decided to let myself go and ran faster and stronger. Before long I had raced ahead of Joe – tears on my face, wanting to use my memory to sweep me round. At mile 20 my partner and Joe's wife waved at me, "Where's Joe?" they shouted. I gestured behind me.

Mile 23 and I ran dry of energy – walked a while and then ran again. I had used up my battery too early, but I ran to the dramatic finish. I felt awful that I had broken the pledge to run with Joe and had left him behind.

As I crossed the finish line my phone rang. "Hi Tom, where are you? I've been waiting just through the finish for you."

Joe had overtaken me, though neither of us had seen the other, and my disregard for our plan to run together had paid me back.

Joe and I still run together. He is still faster than me.

MY LITTLE BROTHER AND I
KELLY LANGFORD

My first Great North Run really was a first for me. I had run a couple of half marathons before, but as my mother lived in Newcastle, I thought I would give a big event a go.

PEOPLE, HELICOPTERS, CAMERAS AND HOSPITALITY

Race day and mother, my brother and I made our way to the city centre. This was certainly a bigger event than the local, Cornish halves I had done with barely 200 runners. People, helicopters, cameras, and hospitality, I was almost dizzy with it all.

Mostly because I couldn't navigate anywhere else, we ended up pretty much at the start line for the masses. I ducked under the tape and waited. There were 15 minutes or so until the start. I had read up on the event and knew people often wore a top layer to be discarded when the race began. Well, I didn't have a lot of running gear, and what I was wearing was my nicest joggers and hoodie, but as mother was there, she could take my clothes.

Less than 10 minutes and I was wondering if I needed to make a break for a toilet. People were emerging from trees in all directions and I wasn't sure where the toilets were. I decided it was my brain playing tricks on me as happens at the start line of every race. Then mother announced she needed the toilet and would be back soon. I hoped she wouldn't miss me starting.

MY 11-YEAR-OLD BROTHER WAS STILL STANDING RIGHT NEXT TO ME

I tried to focus on the race now, get my head in the game, would I get that sub two hour PB I was dreaming of. Two minutes to go. Better take my kit off, hurry up mother. Arghhhhh, I hadn't even noticed my 11-year-old brother was still standing right next to me, exactly where mother had left him. I frantically searched the thousands of people for mother, but she was not there, or I was not seeing her.

SHOULD I LEAVE HIM?

Less than a minute to go. Right, what was I going to do. I was going to run, I am a runner, I did not come all this way not to run. Should I leave him? Surely, she would be back any second, he wouldn't be on his own for long, and he wasn't really on his own anyway, there were I don't know how many thousands of spectators here. She'd never find him. I couldn't leave him!

I pulled him under the tape, took my hoodie off and gave him a sleeve to hold – 'do not let go of this'. One more desperate look for mother. I knew she was not coming, and we were off. What would she think when she came back, and he was not there? Would she alert the police? That was something to worry about after. Now my little brother and I had the Great North Run to complete in our rather too heavy to run jogging bottoms. What amateurs.

I never really appreciated that he ran pretty much the whole way and we finished in 2hrs 10mins. We held those sleeves of that hoodie for dear life. There are a lot of people running that race and letting go for a moment could have meant losing him into the sea of runners bobbing along.

We finished and I was expecting an equally furious and relieved mother waiting at the end. When we found her, she airily congratulated us in her 'Patsy from Absolutely Fabulous' way. I asked what had happened to her at the start?

'Well, on my way to the toilets I bumped into Cain Dingle and the cast from Emmerdale'.

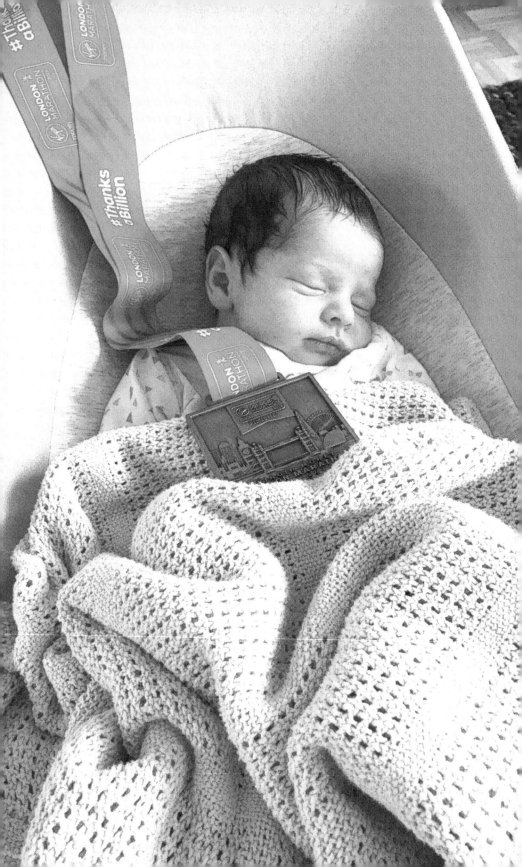

BABY ON BOARD
SALLY RAMSDEN

In April 2019 I had the great news of a positive pregnancy test, although it came with a bit of a dilemma as this was five days before I was due to run the London Marathon. I've run the race several times before and it's always been special, but this time was even more meaningful as I was raising money for the Stroke Association after my father-in-law had a stroke at the beginning of the year. I still wanted to run but was slightly apprehensive with this new and exciting news.

I FELT HAPPY THAT IT WAS SAFE TO RUN

After seeking advice from midwives, I felt happy that it was safe to run. The day felt even more exciting than usual, but also a bit more daunting, with my little secret. I decided not to look for a particular time but to concentrate on enjoying getting round the course, not least because my partner was worriedly tracking my progress along with my mum, who we hadn't yet put in the know.

I SAW A LADY WITH A BABY BUMP

I was given a confidence boost within the first couple of miles when I saw a lady with a baby bump. I really did enjoy myself and made it all the way round at four weeks pregnant. As it turns out, I also managed to be just 16 seconds off matching my PB, finishing in 3:38:01. Another great London marathon memory!

I raised £1,750 for the Stroke Association. Baby Stan arrived by emergency C-section just before Christmas, meeting his Grandad, who is recovering, early in 2020. This was a lovely moment.

WE'VE JUST INVESTED IN A JOGGING BUGGY

I carried on running until around six months pregnant and picked it up again with regular 5k local routes once Stan was 12 weeks old. We've just invested in a jogging buggy so I'm now looking forward to the two of us continuing our running adventures together.

SCARED OF THE DARK
HELEN WORSFOLD

My proudest running achievement came last year when I ran a 100 mile race. I've been running for about seven years, before that I really had no interest in it at all. In fact, I first started with running around a little lake while my husband ran around a big lake, and I spent the whole time moaning that I didn't like it!

I SAY RUN, THERE WAS PLENTY OF WALKING AND SOME SHUFFLING

I never believed I could run that many miles. I say run, there was plenty of walking and some shuffling and just trying to keep putting one foot in front of the other. In the end, it was with the support of an amazing crew of my closest friends and family that got me to the finish line. The running community is truly an awesome thing.

I KNEW THIS WAS GOING TO BE ANOTHER WORLD OF HARD

The terror of arriving at the start and seeing all the 'proper runners' hanging about stays with me to this day. Although I'd managed 70 miles in a 24 hour event a couple of years before, I knew this was going to be another world of hard. In the months preceding the race, I'd run a marathon and a 50 mile race which I'd recovered from much faster than I thought I would, and so figured if I was going to do it that was the time.

IT STARTED TO GO DARK

I got through the first 40-45 miles without too much trouble, but then it started to go dark. I'm really not a big fan of solo running in the dark, in fact I'm scared of the dark. I'd planned to meet up with my friend at just past the 50 mile mark and she was going to run with me through the night (she is a really good friend!). I was behind schedule though and she'd been waiting for me for hours, and it had got dark before I made the check point where she was. When I finally made it, I was thinking, I want to pull out, I'm never going to be able to do this. I ate some pasta threw it back up, I was freezing and felt dreadful. But there were my friends all waiting in the dark for me, willing me on, so I had a word with myself and off we went into the night.

I HAD THE SECOND SERIOUS WORD WITH MYSELF

We were walking by this time, and not fast and it turned out that the caffeine drink which was making me feel so much better was a diuretic – so many loo stops! And squatting was not easy. At some point after seeing a 'Chinese dragon' (woman with a foil blanket round her legs so it turns out), we figured out I wasn't going to make the cut off of 30 hours if I didn't speed up. Not what you need to hear about 70 miles in. So, I had the second serious word with myself, ate some iced gems and sped up.

I FINISHED 20 MINUTES UNDER THE CUT OFF

My feet were agony by this point – so many blisters and my hands had swelled up like sausages which was a source of much amusement to my crew (and me to be fair). But the sun had come up and it made me feel so much better in myself. A blister popped about 98 miles in on a rutted field and I couldn't stop crying, but everyone willed me on, and I was so determined to finish I blanked it all out. My whole crew, including my husband and stepdaughter, were at the end and I cried so many happy tears. I finished 20 minutes under the cut off and I was 4th from last and I couldn't have been happier. I'll not be rushing to do it again though... but never say never...

THANK YOU PARIS
ANDREA SANDERS-REECE

At my 50th birthday party I announced that I intended to run a marathon before I became too old and my arthritis too painful. Once I'd said it out loud to my family and friends, I knew that I would do it. Before that, my running had been minimal and ad hoc, my shoes a size or two too big, and my clothing totally inappropriate. My mother was bewildered.

The first hurdle to my marathon ambitions was to join a local running club. I had been nervous about this as running clubs always appeared as places for really good runners, not people like me. However, everyone I met was incredibly supportive and kind.

I was accepted for the Paris Marathon in April 2006 and my training started in earnest. Gradually I built up my mileage to 50 miles a week, with my longest run around 22 miles. My technological support was a basic watch, a piece of string and my A-Z.

Here is a section from my journal about the Paris Marathon:

Day before: The UN Friendship run is a great way to get into the atmosphere and to shake out some of the fears of a first marathon. Ended up running about seven miles in total, obviously not recommended, three or four is sufficient. Felt bouncy and ready for the big day.

Clothing: Cotton shorts with pockets for my hotel key (designed more for holidays than marathons but they worked for me), hanky and a few mints, white running vest, M&S socks and undies (including a 'substantial' pair of knickers to keep my glutes warm), Asics Gel Nimbus running shoes, sunglasses.

Fuel: Night before – squid ink pasta with seafood sauce, salad, chocolate mousse; breakfast – cereal with extra banana and raisins plus cup of black coffee; during marathon – water which I carried to keep warm (cold water gives me tummy ache); afterwards – rare steak and glass of red wine.

Pain: At around mile 20 I had a searing pain in one of my right toes, so bad I thought I should stop, but carried on. Later back at my hotel I realised that one of my toenails had pushed out of its bed and through the skin of my toe about a centimetre down. I was amazed that the pain wasn't worse and that I could still walk, let alone run.

I had absolutely no concept of what 37,000 runners crammed into Avenue des Champs-Élysées would be like and when I first saw the ocean of people I was completely horrified. Images of school assemblies and feelings of claustrophobia flooded over me and inside the tightness in my throat threatened to strangle me.

It had never entered my head that I needed to arrive early, I thought 15 minutes or so before the start was plenty of time. I'd imagined I'd pop to the loo and then line up with the other runners, just as I had in shorter races – it was the sheer number that sent me into a panic.

Andrea Sanders-Reece in the centre

SHOUTS OF ALLEZ, ALLEZ

I don't remember hearing a gun or hooter just the sound of softly shuffling feet and shouts of 'allez, allez'.

It took five minutes to get to the start line and chip mats, then the crowd of runners thinned leaving space to run and the early downward slope made it easy to get into a comfortable stride and rhythm. This was it. I was running a marathon – the very thing I'd trained and planned for months and held a secret wish to do ever since that first London marathon back in 1981. 3 hours, 35 minutes and 54 seconds later, with the substantial medal dangling around my neck, I was so thrilled and excited to have completed my first marathon.

That was the start of my running life. I went on to run another seven marathons, and discovered a love for running shorter distances, much shorter!

At my first club, Mornington Chasers, I hold every distance record in the W55 + age group from 100m to 10 miles and have won British Masters Championships in 800m (indoor), 1500m (indoor and outdoor) and 3000m (indoor). In 2011, I ran the fastest track mile in the UK in my age group. My biggest achievement was to win the International Triathlon Union World Championship Sprint Duathlon in the W60 Age Group in 2015 in Adelaide (beating the Australians on their home turf).

I continue to race and now coach too at my relatively new club, Serpentine, helping others realise their own running dreams, from racing to – most importantly – enjoying the freedom that running brings.

FINDING MYSELF
CORY WHARTON-MALCOLM

I started running back in 2006 when I was uninspired and overweight. To be honest with you, after years of leading a relatively sedentary lifestyle I only signed up for the London Marathon because other people thought I couldn't do it. So, I did. It was seven hours of agony due to overeating and undertraining, but I finished.

I remember at mile eight thinking to myself how on earth am I going to finish this? I have more than 18 miles to go and I am spent, it's raining, I'm cold, I'm hungry, I'm thirsty, I need the toilet. Stop and go home. These were the messages that replayed constantly in my head. But the one message that would sneak its way in from time to time was keep going, remember, they don't think you can do it, one more step.

I took one more step till I crossed the finishing line in the pouring rain, crying my eyes out, and I didn't even know why. Of course, it hurt, but that wasn't why I was emotional. I had finished and somewhere on the road I had done more than found my running style, I had found myself.

As time passed, I ran more marathons and started to find more of myself. Running helped me smile more, travel more, it helped me find happiness, it gave me my job, my girlfriend, my friends, my healthy lifestyle, but most importantly running helped me to find peace. And that peace is priceless.

Running isn't always about the physical.

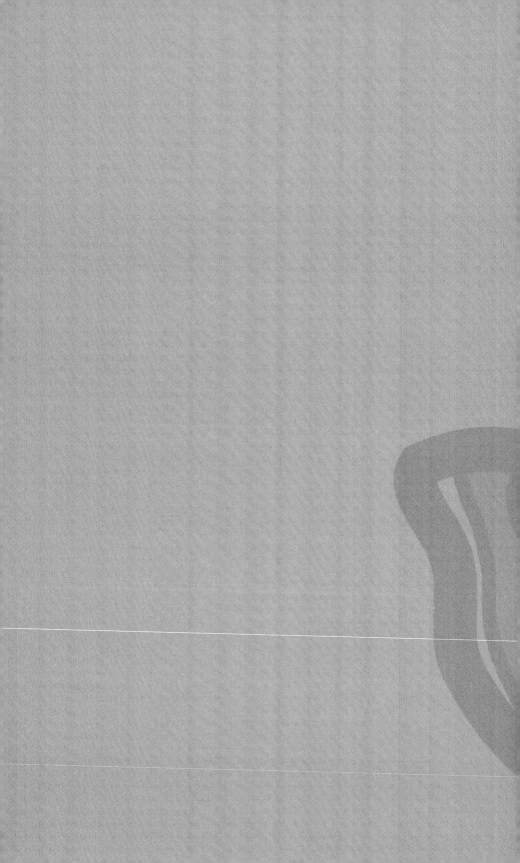

THE COMPETITIVE SPIRIT

RUNNING LIKE HARRY
DAVID SPENCER

When Harry runs there is no track, no course laid out, no mile markers. When Harry runs it is not against the clock. It is not a repetition session and there are no competitors. When Harry runs the distance covered is not noted, no style analysed, no long-term training plan is in motion. When Harry runs, he doesn't know where he is running to or for how long he may run. When Harry runs sometimes, for a second or two, he closes his eyes and he just feels the moment, the movement, the breeze brushing against his cheeks, the looseness of his limbs. When Harry runs it is for the joy of running. When Harry runs it is freedom. Harry is six. He is my grandson. When Harry runs, I also feel what he feels and am thankful.

I CAN REMEMBER EVERY PB

I have been running for 39 years. I've raced at every distance from 50 metres on the track to cross country, road races and marathons. Every step has been measured, long term training strategies analysed, a stopwatch noting every second run. I've recorded every race in detail – place, event, distance, time, and position. I can remember every PB, have run in over 30 countries, and raced on over 100 tracks. I've been exhilarated and frustrated with performances and injuries alike. But now when I run age has crept up on me, and sometimes I feel slow and my steps leaden and heavy. As the years passed, I couldn't fathom how it took me five minutes longer to run a 5km than a decade ago. But I persevered.

Seven years ago, I discovered that to continue running I would need an operation on my ankle. It would be expensive. I decided to have that operation, and as part of my recovery started to learn about strength training. On a whim I tried a 200m track race at Lee Valley. My time was 10% better than the equivalent at 5km.

I HAVE SURPRISED MYSELF

From that moment on I've concentrated on the 400m and 200m, getting stronger and faster, enjoying the tough speed, and the speed endurance sessions. I have surprised myself during this period, winning five M65 and M70 national titles, claiming European relay medals, and breaking the 11-year-old M70 indoor record for 400 metres. (Thanks to my coach Paul McKeown).

JUST OCCASIONALLY, I FEEL LIKE HARRY

I love my training and racing, hard as it is. I love the feeling of being strong again and of surpassing my expectations. When I run, occasionally, just occasionally, I feel like Harry. I am 71 but I feel what he feels and am thankful.

THE SILVER LINING
ANNE DOCKERY

It is not often a person is grateful for rather unpleasant news from the doctor but, having been a heavy smoker when younger, at the age of 55 I was diagnosed with the lung condition bronchiectasis. This started me on an amazing adventure that continues to this day and included becoming the World Duathlon Champion in my 70th year (2018). Talk about a runner's high!

RUNNING GROWS ON YOU SLOWLY

Very reluctantly I started running to strengthen my lungs and prevent my condition getting worse. Running grows on you slowly. After several months I grew to appreciate the meditative quality and the energy it generated. I was entered in a hill-ridden cross-country race and, oddly enough, found the ordeal enjoyable, particularly as I won a medal for coming third in my age group. I was hooked.

A whole new world opened up. I was introduced to the amazing camaraderie of the running community and, since moving to Bristol two years ago, I have been quite overwhelmed by the generous support and encouragement of local runners of all ages as I attempted my first track events.

I was a part of the GB gold medal 4 x 400 metre team for the 70-74 year age group at the Malaga World Masters Athletics Championships in 2018. In the same competition, much to my amazement and delight, I won three individual bronze medals in the 800m, 1500m and 5000m. But the best bit was wearing the British vest and being part of that amazing group of athletes of all ages. Such an honour. If I can do this it shows others can too!

THE BEST BIT WAS WEARING THE BRITISH VEST

As you get older you need to find new dreams and goals. With running there is always another little challenge, whether you are trying to complete your first parkrun, knock a couple of seconds off your 800 metres, or simply enjoy a morning run with friends. You can turn anything into a challenge – and that is what I love. It is not about racing; it is about being the best you can be on a specific day. It is about keeping fit enough to enjoy your grandchildren and being able to live independently for as long as possible.

WE MUST STOP AGE BEING AN ARTIFICIAL BARRIER

We must stop age being an artificial barrier that inhibits the desire to be become fitter, stronger, more adventurous. I am probably more willing to have a go at things now than I was in my 40s, and I have never been happier.

Photo courtesy Alex Rotas

RUNNING BEHIND MO FARAH
MOHAMUD AADAN

My name is Mohamud Aadan, Somalian born England and Great Britain international long-distance runner at 5k, 10k and half marathon. I'm 30 years of age and grew up in the West London borough of Hammersmith and Fulham. I am a member of Thames Valley Harriers athletics club.

As a teenage boy, I arrived in this country from Ethiopia where I and my family were residing with no idea what the new future would hold for me on this side of the world. Before I started running, I played football every day and was addicted to it. However, I realised I have a different energy level to that of playing football and I wanted to do more.

MY RUNNING APPETITES WERE NOT BEING SATISFIED

I put comfortable trainers on and started jogging every day. After a couple of months of jogging in my local park, where I normally played football with my friends, my running appetites were not being satisfied. Meanwhile I started searching on the internet for athletics clubs nearby, and luckily I found Thames Valley Harriers. I went to the club house on a Tuesday evening and asked if I could join the club. I was given a membership form to join, I was so excited.

I ran my first competitive event as a junior athlete in November 2008. I still remember it very well, it was a cross country race, the Metropolitan League 8km. It was a hard race to start with as I ran with the senior men to score points for my club.

I NEVER WATCHED THE FINAL STAGE SITTING DOWN

The reason I run is to race and compete with other athletes around the world, and to become a champion. When I was a young boy living in Ethiopia, I used to watch athletics on television. I watched the World Championships, Olympics, Diamond League and so on. Seeing the Ethiopian talent displayed in front of me and winning medals at those big championships moved me a lot. Especially watching Kenenisa Bekele was amazing. My heart moved so fast and I started sweating thinking that I was running, my adrenaline went up as I watched the screen. I never watched the final stage of any distance race sitting down, I was always on my feet jumping and shouting at the same time.

I realised coming to the UK gave me good opportunities, and I started chasing my dream of being a champion one day.

My goals grew bigger as I experienced different levels of competition, from domestic meetings to national championships. Winning medals and getting new titles are very exciting experiences in my athletic carrier. So far, I have won the Middlesex County Championship in cross country, on the track and on the road, and won other

medals in the England championships on the track.

ran for England in the Commonwealth Half Marathon 2018 (team Bronze), and Great Britain & Northern Ireland in the European Cup 10,000m (team Silver) and the World Half Marathon Championships in 2018. It's a great honour and a wonderful experience to wear the Great Britain & Northern Ireland vest.

My ultimate goal is to represent my country in the Olympic Games in 2021, either on the track or on the road.

The running world is so amazing and gave me great opportunities to travel around Europe and Africa. Travelling to high altitude training camps are the most fantastic experience ever, to see the world's top athletes doing what they do best. I made new friends who are very close to my heart, and new training groups and partners at altitude camps in Kenya and Ethiopia.

LEARNING FROM THEM STRIDE BY STRIDE

It is in training camps that I came very close to my role model and national hero Mo Farah and his training partner Bashir Abdi. I wasted no chance to train with them, following them from behind, learning from them stride by stride. This gave me a chance to improve by training with, and learning from, the world's best athletes.

Apart from racing and winning medals and trophies, running has transformed my life. I'm physically and mentally stronger than ever, enjoying health and wellbeing through sport.

I'LL CARRY ON RUNNING
VIC SHIRLEY

In his 70s Vic has won a host of Gold and Silver medals at European and World Masters Championships at distances from 800m to 10k.

When I was very young, I ran all the time everywhere for fun, just like every other youngster who's able to. Everything was a race or a tumble.

When I was at school it wasn't so much fun, I didn't train properly but I was second in the mile race, although my time was only average compared with good 15-year olds.

I SET A NEW MASTERS V75 RECORD FOR THE MILE

The next time I ran on a track was 60 years later. I set a new British Masters V75 record for the mile of 6:11:08 in July 2018 at the Harvey Hadden Stadium in Nottingham. I had only dropped about 30 seconds in 60 years at that distance. Perhaps this slightly slower than usual fall off in performance, from youth to OAP, has allowed me to compete against runners who ran much faster times during their careers than I could have ever done.

I have no running history at all from being 15 until starting again close to 60 when I did the Great North Run to raise funds for Cancer Research. That event led to quite a few local races, many also for charities until one day in Metres to Miles, our local sports shop run by ex-international Julian Moorhouse, I was told I was in the top 10 in the country. I'd no idea what they were

talking about, but of course it was Power of 10. I realised if I trained harder I could probably do quite well by age category at 10ks and half marathons. I also ran six marathons during this period but each one turned from fun, to effort, to pain, which will be familiar to all who do them. I take my hat off to all marathon and ultra-runners. I won my category in Lake Garda, and it was an unforgettable experience to do Amsterdam, Paris, and Prague too. My six marathon results were reasonable by age category (3:32 to 3:45 in my sixties) but my recovery times were far too long, and I realised it was not my distance.

I joined Northern Masters Athletic Club in 2015 which enabled me to try track running and enter international events. I strongly encourage any younger runners who might read this to one day consider age category masters running. If you have a supportive partner or wife, as I have, they may well enjoy watching a track event much more than seeing you set off in a road event and return a long time later. My wife Judy enjoyed the World Masters Championships so much in Malaga she persuaded me to carry on for another year, so I have much to thank her for.

I CROSSED THE FINISH LINE WITH ONE OF MY SONS AND GRANDSON

Running has kept me fit enough, and lucky enough, to run in events with younger relatives and much younger family

Vic Shirley centre

members, including a memorable local half marathon in 2016 when I crossed the finish line with one of my sons and my grandson, 143 years crossing the line.

HOW MUCH FUN SHOULD AN OLD MAN HAVE?

From the camaraderie before marathons to the emotions brought on by The Great North Run, add in the excitement of track racing, then racing in an indoor stadium, and tell me how much fun should an old man have? It's all been amazing, sometimes surreal, often unexpected, and perhaps not quite over yet. I'm hoping to somehow remain fit enough for the next three years to see what the V80 category might bring. While I can lace up my trainers and get out there, I'll carry on running.

YOU ARE REALLY, REALLY SLOW
ANDREAS NORDGREN

I have always been a sports geek.
Ice hockey, football, floorball, and all team sports filled my childhood in Sweden with joy. Later I bet everything on ice hockey and was very close to a successful professional career. In short, I am technically gifted in sports above average. But what about running?

YOU LOOK TERRIBLE WHEN YOU RUN

We go back to spring 1996, when I was 13 years old. I played a football game in my hometown and remember that I did well. I scored a couple of goals and it was a happy guy who jumped into his mom's car after the game. My mother, who has always been a little too honest, turned to me in the car and said: "Good game Andreas, but I've been thinking about one thing. You have very good technique, but you look terrible when you run, you are really, really slow."

I know it was said with good intention and a weird sense of humour, but it stung me like a giant wasp. Before I got out of the car, I had quietly agreed with myself that I would not be that slow guy with a ridiculous running technique.

The day after my manic side kicked in for real. I went to the running track near our house and the strategy I used is probably not to be recommended, but I ran 2.5-3 km every day until the winter started.
The following spring when it was time for physical tests with the ice hockey team, that slow guy suddenly ran 1 km in the track trial in under 3 minutes. Spin the clock forward another year, the ice hockey team hires an experienced athletics trainer to manage the team's running training during the off-season.

I AM MISSING A RUNNER FOR THE 800m TEAM

After one of the infamous 12 x 1km sessions, he took me aside and said: "Andreas, you have a fantastic running technique and are showing times that are at a good competition level. In a few weeks we have the Swedish Youth Championship and I am missing a runner for the 800m team, can you join?" "Of course," I answered.

So instead of being at the high school graduation, I packed myself into a bus with unknown young people and headed for Värnamo.

The team for 3 x 800 ran in fourth place with a time of 6.21. This is the only time I have run 800m for real. The result is still today, 21 years later, the club record in Täby IS Track and Field.

Imagine what a few words can accomplish. Although running is not my main interest today, it has meant a lot to me over the years and has given me many fun memories. I even ran a marathon in Africa. Without those rather mean words from my mom I would certainly not have done that.

Thanks Mom

A MOTHER & DAUGHTER WORLD RECORD
JACQUIE MILLET

It's 5:30 am on a warm June morning and I am in Richmond Park in London about to run a marathon. There's nothing new in that – I have run over 200 of them in the last 10 years. This one is a bit different though. There is no start line, no officials, no supporters. I'm not wearing a number and there is no set route, not even a medal. This is a marathon in Covid times – a virtual marathon.

THE MOST MARATHONS RUN TOGETHER BY A PARENT AND CHILD

One thing that is the same though is that standing next to me is my daughter Camilla. We have done this so often we have earned a Guinness World Record for the most marathons run together by a parent and child. Guinness' rules require us only to start and finish the same event for it to count but in the early days we ran many of them side by side. In recent times, as Cam has got faster, it is more common for us to wish each other luck and for Cam to join the runners nearer the front of the race. Today we are back to running together.

The reason we are here is an email request (we'd like to think it was personal!) from Eliud Kipchoge – the world's greatest marathon runner and hero of ours. We had travelled to Austria last October to watch him run the first ever sub-2-hour marathon. A very special moment. Today's marathon is to raise money for the Lewa Wildlife Reserve near Kipchoge's hometown in Kenya. In normal times the race takes place in the reserve itself and raises much-needed funds to conserve and protect the animals. We were meant to be travelling to Kenya to run it.

It's four months since we ran our last marathon, in Florida – by far our longest time without running the distance for many years. It wasn't meant to be this way. This year was to be an epic year – we were set to run marathons all over the world. We had qualified for Boston, London, Chicago, and New York. We were running Two Oceans in Cape Town, pacing in Limassol, Liverpool, and Milton Keynes, travelling to Riga, and taking part in our favourite race – the Comrades Marathon in Durban. But Covid has decimated the racing calendar, so here we stand in Richmond Park determined to stay positive and enjoy running together.

My marathon journey started ten years ago when I was 57 years old. I was always interested in running – I enjoyed watching the Olympics and the London Marathon, but never dreamed I could take part. I'd never been overweight but apart from occasional hill walking hadn't done any real sport. A health scare resulted in me deciding to look after myself and get a personal trainer. When he suggested I try running, I never looked back. Cam came to watch my first few marathons and after a bit of persuasion decided to give it a try. It quickly became an important part of our lives.

Someone asked me recently "Haven't you

done enough?" So – why do we keep going? With no crowds, aid stations or other runners, there will be plenty of time today to reflect on what marathon running continues to give us.

The route we have chosen involves four loops of Richmond Park. At this time in the morning the park is magical. With no cars or cyclists, we have it to ourselves along with the deer, green woodpeckers, and parakeets. Marathon running has given us many such experiences. Trail marathons take you through some amazing scenery. City marathons allow unique sightseeing – running round St Mark's Square in Venice completely devoid of tourists, over the Verrazano Narrows bridge in New York, and even through the Mersey tunnel.

Another thing it's given us is the physical and mental fitness to attempt an adventure like this. It gives us confidence that transfers to other things we want to take on. It's a great combination of something that feels good and is good for you.

Marathon running gives us a huge sense of achievement. There's nothing quite like the feeling when you cross the finish line. Two hundred marathons later that's still a special moment. And in big city marathons with thousands of spectators cheering you along the route, though exhausted and maybe even in pain, we feel like celebrities for the day, and often for the rest of the week. Anyone who's met a marathon runner knows that the race doesn't end at the finish line – the celebrations and stories go on for some time!

WE KNOW WHEN TO ENCOURAGE EACH OTHER AND WHEN TO KEEP QUIET

As mother and daughter, we obviously have a very special relationship which has been strengthened by our shared passion. We always have each other to look to when we need some extra support. Having run over 150 marathons together means we know when to encourage each other and when to keep quiet.

One of the things we love most of all is when people tell us how much we've inspired them – to try running, to enter a particular race, or just to push themselves that little bit further. We truly believe that everyone is capable of so much more than they imagine.

And talking about people: that's the best thing about all this. We have met up with runners from all over the world. Some of them we meet briefly in passing on a trip, others we spend time with regularly and we're sure will be lifelong friends.

As the park started to get busier through the morning, we ran past some of those friends and exchanged a wave and a short chat. And as we finished our marathon today, to our surprise they were there to cheer us in.

Who wouldn't want to carry on running marathons?

Jacquie Millet and Camilla Langlands blog: www.thisishowwerun.com

24,901 MILES
JOE CANCELLIERE

The Earth's circumference is about 24,901 miles at the equator. Ignoring the fact that directly following this geographical line would result in more swimming than running, it's my personal goal to run this cumulative distance during my life.

THE LONG RUN HAS BECOME MY CHURCH

I don't need to run fast, just to run far. Whenever I train for a marathon, it seems more than a coincidence that my long runs fall on Sunday. With a congregation of one, the long run has become my church, and running my religion. I'm outside before the sun rises, and the next two to three hours belong only to me, my feet, and the pavement.

HOW MANY MILES LEFT?

For me, running long is a solitary, meditative practice. My mind empties all thoughts and becomes a calculator, keeping a tally of my distance. How many miles have I run? My feet find their cadence, keeping tempo in the morning silence. How many miles left? The sun creeps over the horizon, dawn shifting into day. How many minutes until the next mile? My watch chirps away with each interval. How many miles have I run now? I continue counting in my head, and my legs move me forward until I reach the end. I stretch, I shower, I eat a very large meal, I return to the world and my calculator mind switches back to normal thought until the next run.

Running around the Earth doesn't need to follow a straight line. I run around the world by running wherever I am. It'll still be a couple decades before I complete the journey, but I hope to get there someday. No matter where I've lived or travelled, running is a part of my life. Running on beaches, in forests, on treadmills, in big cities, regardless of location, the miles add to the running total, continuing my personal race around the world.

IT'S ABOUT OTHER PEOPLE TOO

JIM, THE COACH
GRACE WU

I have been racing since I was 12. Back then, in the 1980s, running was so simple, pure, and innocent. A man, Jim, saw me win a low-key school race and told me to meet him and his athletes at a track the following week. There were no DBS criminal record checks, no coaching qualifications, no questions asked.

I tentatively went along and ran with some other kids in a pair of plimsolls and a borrowed pair of spikes for the speedy stuff. He told me to go slower or faster as I passed him each 400m. I didn't really know my splits and I didn't really care. Jim looked after all of that. After training, I'd grab a bag of greasy chips on the way home and did my homework. I trained three times a week and sometimes raced. I raced whatever event Jim told me I should do. I had a laugh. I didn't think about running much. I turned up and just ran. Jim sorted everything out. I won county titles and raced at the All England. I only ran, it was Jim who did all the hard work.

As an adult in their 40s, it's all so complicated. In order to race, I need to implement a logistical plan organised at least a week in advance, and the mental noise on race day is inane and irritating – how painful will it be, what if I trip over, what if the babysitter doesn't show up and the kids burn the house down whilst I'm racing? My Garmin is synced to my mobile, I upload data, I download training plans. I have shoes for different surfaces and distances. Splits are calculated and

Grace is left and Jim on the right

memorised. School cotton socks have been replaced by high tech compression ones. Greasy chips at the end of training? A specific carb protein shake is more likely.

From this complicated and elaborate running approach, have I achieved as much as I did as a child? Absolutely not if we're looking at the results pages. Maturity, however, has taught me about human kindness – the dedicated race organisers, marshals, and of course, Jim. The man who gave up so much of his free time and who taught me about the ups and downs of racing and life.

As a teenager, I didn't value Jim enough, nor the overwhelming generosity from so many people. But with age I appreciate all of this and, for me, I think that's more important than winning championships.

OLD PHOTOS
ALEX ROTAS

Alex challenges stereotypes about ageing through photography.

I started photographing older athletes when I was 60. I realised there weren't any images of older sporty people circulating in the media. I did an internet search and once that word 'old' went in, you just got pictures of older people slumped in chairs. I knew this was only part of the picture, and maybe even only a small part at that. Who'd want to get old if this was what lay ahead?

As a sporty person myself, I was very aware that there were plenty of us out there and that there was a whole other side to this 'ageing' coin. It seemed to me that some positive and joyful imagery could fill a real gap and encourage people to look forward to getting older, rather than dreading it.

I took photography lessons (I didn't have a camera at the time) and started attending national and international sports competitions. I was particularly drawn to the Masters track and field athletes. I'd never been a runner or an athlete myself, but had played competitive tennis all my life. I was blown away by what I was seeing when I started photographing these athletes.

As a tennis player, you can often hide your lack of physical fitness behind your racket skills. A killer-dropshot is a great one to have up your sleeve. But with the athletes, there was no hiding. You took yourself to the start line and boom, the gun went off

and it was just you, your body and your physical and mental fitness that got you to the finish line.

I never imagined I'd be seeing people in their 60s, 70s, 80s and 90s do what I saw them doing. They made me completely recalibrate my sense of what the ageing body is capable of. I thought that if I was surprised, then others would be too. I really wanted to get my pictures out to a broader audience and make people think again about what getting older is all about.

FULL OF LIFE, FULL OF JOY

I found the athletes I was photographing to be full of life, full of joy. They were inspirational on every level. You could see they loved competing and relished their physicality. But they were part of a wonderfully joyful and supportive community too. I wanted to try to get all of this across in my photographs.

COACHING MUSINGS
DAVID CHALFEN

Once a degenerative injury and approaching forty took its toll, it was clear that there was only one way my results were going to head. It seemed likely that I might do better as a coach than as a runner (not much to surpass, admittedly). Running performance has a strong genetic element which isn't shared by coaching, though one shouldn't lose sight that in both you are still largely in control of your own destiny and can make as much or as little of it as you choose.

CAREFUL ABOUT WHICH RUNNERS YOU FORGE LINKS WITH

You learn gradually that coaching will be more fulfilling if you are careful about which runners you forge links with. I've been lucky to know some wonderfully impressive people whose running achievements are just one small part of why I admire them. They are people you would truly want on your team in life generally, never mind them tanking round a 5.2 mile leg in the Southern 12 stage relay.

EVERY ATHLETE IS A CASE STUDY OF ONE

You learn early on that every athlete is a case study of one. Although you might suggest that both the driven, national level whippet, and the age grouper striving to break 3.45 for the marathon at some stage do, say, 7x1200 metres or a 12 mile strong progression run, it will certainly help to be aware of where and why such challenges fit into their varying lives and goals.

Coaching musings often drift towards the old chestnut about whether it's an art or a science. It is surely, obviously, and always a combination of both, which is maybe why coaches' backgrounds and preferences cover such a wide range.

SOMETHING OR SOMEONE WILL ALWAYS BE AROUND TO CAST DOUBT

It's as well never to be convinced that you are much good at coaching, because no matter how much evidence there might be to suggest this is so, something or someone will always be around the corner to cast doubt on it. In years when I have coached seven or eight of the Top 100 guys in the London Marathon, which includes the UK Championships, almost inevitably another coachee in the same event will have a disappointment. Picking up the pieces after a setback is harder and takes longer than celebrating the achievements. And whilst a long term batch of testimonials is greatly reassuring, one that has really stuck in my memory (as it was – honestly – rather far off the normal spectrum) was the feedback that I was "The most demotivating coach I've ever met and I've told all my friends and family not to be coached by you." Ouch.

I'd contest that volunteer coaching isn't necessarily as altruistic or "giving" as is sometimes depicted. We do it because we like it; we like the people, we like the process, we like the spectacle of competitive sport, we like the results, we like our efforts being validated and, yes, we like showing what smartarses we can sometimes be. We don't like standing in the cold biting rain, and the weird fact that mankind still hasn't invented an umbrella that doesn't break in a strong wind on Hampstead Heath; or the frustration when a runner is injured (especially if they got injured skiing, though don't get me started on this), or missing a race because the sodding North Circular traffic seems parked across North London, but it's almost unheard of for a coach to retire just because of such annoyances. British distance legend Jon Brown (twice 4th in Olympic Marathons, now a leading coach in New Zealand) once said of runners' nutrition "It's very important, but very overrated." I think one might say the same of coaches. See, I said we are smartarses.

Photo courtesy Maren Urner.

117

GUIDING A BLIND RUNNER
PHIL BRADBURN

Imagine you really want to run, but you need an extra pair of eyes to enjoy what you love so much. I know a great blind runner called Louise who I guided on part of a 24-hour ultra-marathon relay. A friend, Maria, wanted to find out more about this often-hidden side of running, so I brought them together.

THEY ARE RUNNERS, FIRST AND FOREMOST

Louise, as with many visually impaired and blind runners, is just like you and me. They are runners, first and foremost. They love running and occasionally they don't, but most of all they just want to run, and meet someone who will run with them.

LOUISE HELD THE INSIDE OF MY RIGHT ARM

From our rendezvous at London's Liverpool Street Station we headed to Spitalfields market. Finding a nice stretch of super-flat pavement, devoid of market traders and tired commuters, we set down our bags. Louise and I left Maria with the bags and ran 400 metres out and back to show Maria how easy it was. Louise held the inside of my right arm lightly and reminded me not to squeeze her arm against my ribs. We made it back without any problems at all.

Now it was Maria's turn. Louise tried to take Maria's arm and missed, instead grabbing her shoulder. Thankfully,

Maria saw the funny side and the two of them managed to link up. They headed off, tentatively at first, but soon picked up speed. Louise is quite the speed merchant, and both of us had the feeling she often likes to go faster.

I CAN SMELL A STARBUCKS

First test run over, we headed off, Louise running with me. It felt natural. As we ran, I described some of the views, the sights, and gave a few instructions along the way (high kerb and high step were quite common ones). At one point Louise piped up "I can smell a Starbucks." Maria and I couldn't even see one. It was only on the second lap that we noticed it.

It wasn't long before the witty quips started to flow. Not from me, but from Louise. Her sense of humour is dry, cutting, and takes no prisoners. She teased me several times; mostly about my poor sense of direction and tendency to get lost.

We ran for a couple of miles, zigzagging around pedestrians, bollards, across roads, past crowded pubs. Maria and I each took an opportunity to guide while the other ran on ahead to scout out a path of least resistance through the crowds. Louise confided that 'urban' running isn't really her thing, she much prefers quieter parks. But she said that she enjoyed it all the same. I suspect, given what I know about her pace (which she is very modest about), Louise just wanted to put her foot to the floor in a big way.

From left to right: Phil, Louise and Maria

According to Louise, the biggest fear of a guide runner is that they will do something wrong. They will trip over the other runner. They will misjudge a gap and run their guidee into a lamppost. They will get them run over by the 88 bus. None of these terrible things happened the night that we met for a run. We didn't even get lost.

DON'T TALK TOO MUCH

So, what's hard about guide running? Nothing. It is easy to do, and like most things, the more practice you get, the better you become. Everyone has their special preferences – whether they run like Louise with her hand on your arm, or with a tether, or simply using the guide as a, well, visual guide. The other tip is don't talk too much. As a guide, I only mention the things that make a difference, such as tree roots, but not a barely perceptible undulation in a completely flat piece of tarmac.

At the end of the evening as we were enjoying a coffee before heading off our different ways, Maria said she would be happy to guide Louise in future – if she will have her – which was a brilliant result. It was lovely to see runners helping each other. If you get the opportunity to guide for someone, take it. It is a great experience and will give you a new perspective on running.

POSTCODE RUNNING
CIARAN THAPAR

Over the weekend I went for a jog through the small park near my flat in Brixton, South London. There I passed an 18-year-old whom I mentor. I'll refer to him as Carl. Carl was jogging too. We slowed to greet one another, then I veered north, towards Kennington. Carl stayed to complete laps of the park, which is next to his housing estate.

The difference in our jogging routes – Carl's closed and repetitive, mine open and free – might seem unremarkable. But it marks out an invisible line of socioeconomic and racial inequality that would divide us if we hadn't met nearly five years ago at a local community centre. I am free to go to Kennington whenever I like, but Carl is not. A territorial rivalry exists between young, predominantly black men in north Brixton and Kennington. Carl knows that by stepping beyond a certain point he is risking his life. By the age of 16 he had dodged knives. He has felt a bullet graze his ear.

He inherited a constant state of insecurity from olders at a young age. He didn't have a choice.

If a moped carrying a masked rider passes Carl, his eyes dart. If he sees a group of unfamiliar adolescent boys approaching, his fist clenches and his heart races. If a car decelerates nearby, Carl suspects it to be undercover police. He is in constant survival mode. Like most middle-class adults in gentrifying areas of London, I can access leisure and visualise opportunities. Carl internalises judgment, surveillance, and trauma. I feel safe; he navigates a warzone. Normally, out of lockdown, I can retreat every few weeks to visit my family in the suburbs. He barely ventures outside Brixton. In other words, Carl and I experience unequal versions of the city.

From the article "Fear, fury and a failed state: Black people are hurt and killed by police without repercussions in the UK too" from the September 2020 issue of British GQ.

AHMAUD ARBERY RIP

CELESTINE AGBO

runner's tribute.

am a runner not a mugger
am a runner not a mugger
am a runner
ot a mugger
n my heart I am free
n my head I am not
urtains twitch
ingers itch
rab your child hold your bag
utside the track
 BLACK MAN running
ould never be
 good sign
ike the wind my feet take wing
all the cops or get the gun
 is my right
o
hoot him dead
ne less Negro in my yard
an truly be
ot a bad thing
was a runner not a mugger
was a runner not a mugger
was a runner not a mugger
our life matters so did mine

n February 23, 2020, Ahmaud Arbery, an unarmed
-year-old African-American man, was pursued and
tally shot while jogging in Glynn County, Georgia.

ural by Marvin Weeks.
hoto courtesy Judson McCranie, Wikimedia Commons.

RUNNING INTO FRIENDS
STACEY TASKER

I first heard of parkrun from a running club, who thought it would be perfect for me, as I only wanted to run once a week, not far, and lacked a competitive streak. It was at a low time in my life as I had just moved to London and had few friends, only colleagues from work.

So in January 2014 my daughter and I turned up at Richmond parkrun in football shirts (so for a while I was called Lampard!) and like the world over, we were really touched by the whole experience and became immediate converts. One day walking back to the car, I was chatting to two parkrunners and they kindly said "Why don't you come and join our group for coffee?"

THERE'S NO SHORTCUT TO MAKING FRIENDS

The following week I nearly didn't join them again, as I still felt shy, but I'm so glad I overcame that hesitancy, as what a total lifeline that group has proved to be. There's no shortcut to making friends – friendship evolves through shared experience. We've had so much fun as we've supported each other through no end of antics (but also personal highs and lows), invariably involving running, often batons, usually getting lost, lots of WhatsApp texts, photos, laughter, food and drink.

But never have this special group been more important to me than when I was struck down with Covid-19. I was totally floored by the virus, in lots of debilitating pain, high fever, couldn't eat, and living alone made everything more difficult and worrying. But Pembroke Athletica (as we are fondly known) came to the rescue and along with my darling daughter, nursed me back to health virtually, including dropping a range of items at my door from medical to food to isotonic water, a webcam (for my daughter to keep an eye on me) and when I was getting better, running past my house to wave to me from the towpath.

Who would have thought that running would prove to be such a vital bridge in my life, especially as I'm always whinging as I run along, no matter how short the distance.

FREEMAN, HARDY & WILLIS
JOHN & PAUL SMITH

We are three brothers living in East London who have run together most Saturday mornings since 1987, when one of us moved to Hackney, within easy reach of the other two already resident in Forest Gate. A much-loved uncle had already labelled us "Freeman, Hardy & Willis" as a collective, not because anybody ever bought any running shoes there, he just had a way with that sort of terminology.

Creatures of habit, the run has almost always been the same: start on the Capel Road side of Wanstead Flats; round the periphery past the Holly Tree pub and the reconfigured ponds; across past the back of the houses on Bushwood and round coming out by the tennis club; over the road to Wanstead Park (a real Epping Forest jewel); up the only hill alongside the golf course, then down to the lake and round; out of the Park and back in at the entrance by the tea hut and on until we leave it at the edge of the Aldersbrook estate; up the road to the Flats and across back to Capel Road. In all a total of six to seven miles in very approximate times that have increased markedly over the years, but who cares?

While the route itself has varied little, we have certainly seen a lot of other changes over the years. The funfair and the occasional circus still turn up on the Lakehouse Road side of the Flats for some Bank Holidays, although we no longer pass strolling elephants, camels and llamas taking a break from the ring. The free-ranging cattle of Epping Forest are also

From left to right: Paul, John and Steve Smith

long gone, but now and again we still see one or two trucks holding hundreds of racing pigeons awaiting their release for a long race back to the North. At one stage we each had a dog and so we ran on a three-men and their dogs' basis, killing two birds with one stone, as they say. Fortunately, they didn't ever bother the elephants.

A recent change has been the arrival of the parkrun, with all ages, types and abilities running two circuits of the Bushwood side of the Flats. While we probably share no more than 50 metres of that run, it's a real pleasure to see such participation and enthusiasm on a weekly basis.

While the dogs are long gone, as are Freeman, Hardy & Willis, we brothers are still running that well-trodden route, come rain or shine, mud or ice. A time to run, relax and socialise, to chat about the week gone by, the days ahead, the lives we are living and the world and his wife. And the weather. But rarely how long it is taking us.

RUNNING CONNECTS ME TO THE WHOLE WORLD

KATI JAEGER

I'm 51 and I live in Rostock, Northern Germany.

Why did I start running? I had cancer in 2014, got through it well and started to think about how to continue. I was sporty as a child and so I started walking. My legs quickly told me to run, not to walk. And so, my body started to move.

Then suddenly a friend said I should register for a race. I laughed at him and ran my first race two months later. Almost 10k. Hey, that's fun! So, the next run. And then my friend said: Half marathon next, go! I said he was crazy. But I soon took the next step. And so it went on. Six marathons so far.

In a Facebook post, a New Zealand runner wrote about her fear of having breast cancer. I answered, now we are friends. I met her Japanese running friend in Chicago in 2018 and still know him. I got to now a Swede briefly in Chicago at the start, and a runner from Hong Kong after the marathon. Since then I've seen everyone somewhere in the world. You talk about your success, you plan together.

Everything has collapsed this year. No more official runs. For me Tokyo, Berlin and Rostock cancelled, as well as a few smaller runs. I love Ragnar Relays. For the first one in Germany in autumn 2018, we put a team together. Today we are still close friends, 12 runners from all parts of Germany. Our team events are cancelled. So, I had to come up with something.

FROM ALL AROUND THE WORLD ALL RUNNING AT THE SAME TIME

I wanted to start a race with friends from around the world all running at the same time. Because of the time difference, it is of course a bit more difficult. So, I came up with the EASTER World Run.

Every participant, no matter where in the world, should run from 09:00 to 10:00 in the morning. Six hundred and fifty people took part, from New Zealand to Alaska. I did the last time zone myself because there was no runner available. My team from Germany took part, we are not incorrectly called "The Best". It was really mega. Especially when I ran the last hour, through the night, right through the corona lockdown. My trainer and coach from the USA ran with me at the same time in his home country. Just the thought

of how great it was that so many runners had followed my Facebook call in just one week still fascinates me and gives me goosebumps as I write this.

WE RUN VIRTUALLY AROUND THE BALTIC SEA

I was able to implement my ideas wonderfully with this run. I just loved to connect these many people who have the same hobby. I got a lot of nice words for which I am still very grateful. And they motivated me to organise a worldwide run. Since June 1st, 260 runners in 13 teams have been running in the GREAT Race Around the Baltic Sea. The condition for each team was that at least five different nationalities had to be represented amongst 20 runners. My team "The GREAT" consists of runners from 20 countries. I know half of them personally. We run virtually around the Baltic Sea and have until the end of August to do it. That is 7,080k, about 27k per runner per week. I coordinate the whole thing. I show the teams where they are on the map. I motivate them and have the greatest fun myself. Connecting people is so easy! Especially if they are runners.

Running is the greatest thing for me. Nothing is boring in my life anymore. Running connects me to the whole world. It doesn't just make me healthy. I now have vacation spots until the end of my life. And that's a great feeling. I look forward to everything that comes next.

WITH A LITTLE HELP FROM A FRIEND
JOE BEST

I will never run a marathon. This is what I said, and I said it often. I managed a busy performance and rehabilitation clinic in London with a lot of my clients being runners. I was a young, fit and somewhat healthy 20 something man, playing lots of rugby, exercising on a nearly daily basis and watching runners in the street thinking, "That doesn't look fun, it actually looks quite hard, why are you doing that to yourself!"

PARIS HERE WE COME

Then two close friends from my rugby team decided that, with no running experience, they would enter the South Coast Challenge, a 50km race from Arundel to Brighton. I helped train the guys and will never forget the sense of achievement I felt watching them cross the finish line, and I had done nothing! I was immensely proud, and a lot of money was raised for Cancer Research, well done guys. At lunch time the next day the parents (after a few Proseccos) announced that they had loved watching the guys run, it was much better than rugby as you didn't have to watch it through your fingers through fear of someone being injured. Thirty seconds later my Mum's best friend informed us that her birthday was on April 12th and the Paris Marathon was on April 14th. Who wants to go to Paris? We looked up charity spots, applied, paid, place confirmed. Paris here we come!

It was time to get serious, training starts now. I have trained a lot of runners in the past and know how difficult it is to train without a target time. But what is achievable? I had run my first half marathon in 1:49 after a game of rugby, was happy running a 1:45 around the streets, so 3:30 should be possible right? The challenge I had was the unknown. I knew that five minutes a kilometre was achievable, but how long for? I would need to work out how to pace a race for the first time so the wheels don't fall off, what would I do? I was understandably nervous, and that is when my Knight in Shining Armour appeared, the man whose name is on the cover of this book. Jerry.

I had trained Jerry on and off over the years, mostly towards the business end of a big race to give him that extra edge. Jerry is a very experienced runner, runs multiple marathons every year and did his 3:26 PB age 65. When Jerry heard I was doing Paris and aiming for 3:30, his response was, 'I am running the Seville Marathon a few weeks before but I'm happy to do Paris with you and pace you for 3:30, it will be fun'. That was music to my ears.

It started as most marathons do, with panic. The tube station we had been told 'was 100% open and running in the morning' was indeed closed. I meet Jerry and we get close to the start line when we notice there is no entry to the starting pen. Thousands of people are frantically looking for gaps between eight-foot-high fencing. Fortunately, someone with a great deal of strength ripped two of the fence panels

erry left and Joe right

apart and we streamed through towards the start, but we are late and find ourselves bundled into the 3:45 not 3:30 wave.

It took a while to get up to pace as most big races do, but we hit a decent speed and the first few kilometres ticked by nicely. We hit the 10k sign, but had actually done 10.2k, something I hadn't put much prior thought into. With a quick calculation I realised that would be nearly 1k extra over the marathon, which we hadn't accounted for in our pacing. Jerry informed me that we were slightly behind pace and would need to pick up a little, which we did. I will never forget the feeling of hitting the halfway stage seven seconds off our target time, sitting on Jerry's shoulder the whole

way. Seven seconds in 1 hour and 45 minutes of running, with an adjusted journey to the start line, a delayed start time, weaving between people to keep pace, Jerry had got us to halfway just seven seconds off pace. I mean, Kipchoge used a car in cruise control on a closed road and ran in a dead straight line to achieve that!

WE GOT TO 32K AND JERRY INFORMED ME THAT IT WAS TIME FOR ME TO GO

This gave me all the confidence I needed. We got to 32k and Jerry informed me that it was time for me to go, with Seville Marathon still in his legs he needed to slow a little due to fatigue and I would need to go it alone. Please Jerry no. But we had agreed the day before that if one of us was fatiguing it was the duty of the other to press on.

The next 10k was the hardest running I have ever done; they say that a marathon is a 20 mile run with a six mile race at the end and now I know why. I crossed the finish line in 3:29:26, head in my hands almost in tears. I wanted to wait for Jerry who subsequently finished three minutes later, but an incredibly angry Frenchman rightly pointed out that waiting on a finish line of a marathon wasn't a smart idea. We met in a café afterwards for a couple of Heinekens and they were the best beers I have ever had. Without Jerry I have no doubt I would not have achieved my goal, and for that I will be forever grateful.

RUNNING FOR LOVE
CHARLIE THUILLIER

On a lovely hot day, running along a track in Regents Park with my brother Harry, I laid eyes on a beautiful blonde lady running in front. Holy smokes, I thought.

It was May 2016. We were at an event for my company Oppo Brothers ice cream, running before a picnic in the park – and I had just spotted Rosy.

She was being chatted up by a chap who seemed to be doing rather well. I ran a little faster and got within ear shot, too close to be socially acceptable, but it was worth the risk. The very good looking, evidently clever, charming boy mentioned he wanted to join a running club, and the lady running by his side replied "Oh you must come down with me, I'm part of Clapham Chasers – love it!" I needed to speak with her before that went much further.

I ONLY KNEW WHAT SHE LOOKED LIKE FROM BEHIND!

The running finished and we settled down for the picnic, but I lost sight of her, and with panic I realised I only knew what she looked like from behind! (I would soon get used to running behind Rosy, trying to keep up). You can imagine the relief when I saw the same figure jogging off to the toilets in the park. This was my opportunity. I made my apologies to the group of potential consumers I was pitching to and made my move, intercepting her just as she was leaving the toilet (a tad on the creepy side but needs must). I tentatively tried to make conversation.

I EXPLAINED I WANTED TO JOIN A RUNNING CLUB

"Hi" I said, "I'm Charlie," "Oh you're the one with the lovely puppy?" "Yes" I lied, thrilled my brother had brought his four-month-old pup along. I explained I wanted to join a running club, and did she know of one? Silence, until she finally said "Er, yeah. I'm part of Clapham Chasers, you could probably come down?"

Bloody bingo. OK, not the willing offer the other chap had received, but it would do!

A MONTH LATER WE HAD BOOKED OUR FIRST DATE

A week later at Battersea Athletics Track I was trying my hardest to impress. It seemed to work, as a month later we had booked our first date. (The month was my fault. I was playing hard to get.)

With friends the night before I proudly announced that I had a date I was very excited about. 'This lady is golden' (or words to that effect) I think I said. One friend, Tim, enquired as to my plans.

I said we were going to have a picnic on Clapham Common, and I'd organised a hamper from a café called 'Tart' that sold amazing tarts. The hamper would overflow with champagne, strawberries, and of course great tarts. I'd even bought a candle, proper champagne flutes, and a portable speaker for some smooth jazz. A picnic had never been so meticulously planned.

im raised his eyebrows before suggesting take a tuna cucumber sandwich to halve nstead. "That way if she's a dud you can inish your mouthful and get out of there."

hank God, I didn't listen to him.

KNEW SHE WAS THE ONE

'osy and I chatted and laughed until the un went down. I was totally bowled over. knew she was the one.

'rom that point on we were inseparable. ive weeks later, on the final day of our oliday in Lake Como, we climbed up Monte Legnone, a 2700m mountain. t is so steep that at many points you are raversing with ropes, not clipped on, vith a big drop either side. Of course, Rosy thought it would be great fun to

run up the mountain where possible.

All was going well until my mobile rang and I was informed of a big problem at work. Rosy was upset I was working on our last day and paying little attention to the beauty around us, so she ran faster to get away from me and my noisy work conversation. In turn, I ran even faster trying to keep up. We eventually reached the top in a sweaty mess. Rosy was petrified and shaking from sprinting through the steep bits. But it remains one of the best holidays we have ever had.

Two years later, on our anniversary, it was clear what I had to do. I surprised Rosy with a trip back to Monte Legnone, turned my phone off, and proposed at the top of the mountain.

I RUN SO LITTLE MARK CAN
IAN JONES

I am just a normal family guy with a wife and three children who works a demanding full-time job.

Five years ago, a friend asked me to join them at a parkrun. I was fit, but not a runner and had never run at an organised event, other than playing football. Well, I loved it. The diverse backgrounds and abilities took my breath away (or was that the running) and I was hooked. I couldn't wait to go back the next week and even started to train for it.

A short time later a pregnant colleague was diagnosed with cancer. She and her family were devastated, as were the team who work with her. Luckily, the charity Mummy's Star looked after her and supported her through the pregnancy and treatment. I was overwhelmed by the support they gave her and knew I had to pay them back.

In the next 12 months I ran a marathon and a 24 hour obstacle course race in the Nevada Desert in which I came 96th out of 2,500 runners. I was so proud of my achievement, but even more so for raising over £4,000 for Mummy's Star. This took me far past my comfort zone and I thought I had found my limit. That was until I found out about a two-year-old named Mark Robinson.

Mark was to have his leg amputated due to a bone condition. It was his young wish to be able to play football and run around with his brother and friends. To do this he needed a prosthetic sports blade, not just for now but in different sizes as he grows up. I immediately started looking at new things that would test me whilst raising money for Mark.

I'M GOING TO RUN 100 MILES NON-STOP

Someone asked me 'what do you think is impossible for you to do.' After some hard thinking I said, 'That's it, I'm going to run 100 miles non-stop and call it 'Run So Little Mark Can'.

I set off on a 106 mile run from Leeds to Burscough in Lancashire along the Leeds to Liverpool Canal. I reached the 100 mile mark in 23 hours and 22 minutes and was over the moon to be able to say I had joined the 100 mile club.

I backed this up by returning to America to race the world's toughest 24 hour obstacle course in Atlanta and shocked myself by coming 26th out of 2,500 runners. I couldn't believe what I had achieved in just a few years, but once again the real excitement was when I totted up the sponsorship and found I had raised £3,500 for Mark to put towards his new legs.

MARK GOT HIS FIRST SPRING

A short time later Mark got his first spring. The video of him running down his street was the best thing I had ever seen and brought more than just one tear to my eyes.

AN EXPERIENCE OF A LIFETIME
RICHIE THOMAS

I have always run since I was a teenager, however it was only in my 40s after I retired from rugby that I got into long distance running seriously. I happened to mention to my barber, an ex-professional boxer who ran marathons for charity, that I'd love to run the London Marathon one day. By the following haircut he told me I was in, running for the charity International Care & Relief (which became Build Africa and has merged with Street Child). I've always been passionate about the power of education to lift people from poverty, and so this cause really appealed to me as it built schools in the remote regions of sub-Saharan Africa.

I'VE RAISED OVER £80,000

I ran my first London Marathon in 2002. Since then I have run 35 marathons, including eight ultras. I have also run countless half marathons and competed in 12 sprint triathlons. I ran them all for Build Africa and I have raised over £80,000 for the charity in the last 18 years. In 2005 my daughter and I were privileged to visit the Masindi District of Uganda to open a new school in the remote village of Nyakibete, which I and other runners had funded out of our charitable donations. That was an experience of a lifetime and, when my stamina is low and I'm hitting The Wall, it's the thought of helping such desperate communities which gives me the strength to carry on and finish the race.

In 2009 I ran my first Comrades Marathon (a "Down Run" of 89k) in under 11 hours and earned a Bronze Medal, my proudest running achievement. I ran two further Comrades, and on our second visit my wife and I visited the Ethembeni (Hope) School at Inchanga, just before the half-way point of the race. This is a school for handicapped children who have been rejected by their families. The previous year our hearts had gone out to the albinos who are considered to be "children of the devil" and thrown out by their parents. We collected a whole suitcase of sports hats from work colleagues and friends and gave them out to the children. The following day when I ran past the school during the race the children formed a guard of honour along the route wearing the hats we'd given them. My eyes were full of tears (then and now, just thinking about it) but their happiness in adversity inspired me to finish the race.

SIX MONTHS AFTER MY HEART ATTACK I CROSSED THE LINE IN CHICAGO

Despite my fitness, in April 2013 I suffered a heart attack and had a stent fitted in a coronary artery which was almost blocked. I had to miss the London Marathon that month, but six months after my heart attack I crossed the line in Chicago in under five hours. As directed by my cardiologist I kept my average heartbeat throughout the race safely under 130bpm!

I thought I had put ill health behind me, but in February 2019 I was diagnosed with advanced and aggressive prostate cancer (5+5 on the Gleason Scale). Despite going through cancer treatment, I ran my thirteenth London Marathon that April and raised £2,500 for Prostate Cancer Research. There is no doubt in my mind that running helped me to maintain a positive attitude, kept me fit and psychologically strong, and got me through the horrible experience of cancer treatment.

I FULLY INTEND TO CARRY ON AS LONG AS MY HEALTH ALLOWS

I am still running, but the cancer drugs drain my stamina and so it's much slower and the distances are much shorter. My wife and I have become ambassadors at the local parkun for the Move against Cancer Charity's '5k Your Way' initiative which encourages those living with and beyond cancer to exercise. We run, jog, or walk with cancer sufferers and give them the benefit of our running experiences as they will learn how beneficial running is for their well-being.

Running is an important part of my life and, now I'm in my 60s, I fully intend to carry on as long as my health allows. Hopefully, I'll be able to run another marathon before too long and, who knows, maybe even another Comrades.

COFFEE RUNNERS
CAROLE O'LEARY

Carole started the Coffee Runners in Hackney, East London to combine running with social activity.

The idea came to me when I was working as a personal trainer doing 1:1 sessions from 6-9am for people before work. I wanted to do something social for people who were around after 9am as I wasn't having much interaction doing just 1:1s. So, the idea of a group class with the social element of going for coffee came about. Hackney has a lot of nice coffee shops to choose from.

A VERY SHAKY START

It began in February 2012, after a very shaky start. I had to cancel the first ever Monday session at short notice when I woke up unable to walk properly. I had extremely painful, stiff calves from running the Brighton Half Marathon on the Sunday. This was something I hadn't experienced before and later found out it was because I was pregnant!

Luckily the two ladies who had booked gave me another chance, turning up for the Wednesday session. They stuck at it and six weeks later completed their first 5k parkrun. I'm happy to say those two both still run with me to this day.

The group was set up in the format of Couch to 5k, meeting twice a week and a third run to do as homework, to try and foster independent running. The aim was to show that anyone can do it, you just need to start at the beginning, stick to a programme and make it routine.

DISCOVER THE LOCAL COFFEE SHOPS

The other part was introducing people to the great outdoor spaces to run in their local area, meet neighbours, and discover the local coffee shops.

Each six-week programme ended by taking part in the local parkrun at Hackney Marshes, introducing the group to their local running community network and being able to do a timed run for free. I was always the back marker making sure no one finished alone or last.

At our first parkrun we were last by a mile. They were packing up when we got to the line as it was mainly club runners that all finished in well under 30 mins. We did it around the 35min mark. Now they have a tail walker and 400+ runners, joggers and walkers. Coffee Runners are not the last anymore. We also are part of the community often providing volunteers.

The parkrun was meant to mark the end of the programme, leaving people with a network of running buddies, knowledge of local running routes and of the local running scene. You've learnt to run, we have done a 5k, I'm very proud, see you later. However, people signed up to do the six-week programme again, and then again, until it became two groups, a beginner and an improver.

e have gone on to do 10ks, weekend
nning holidays, numerous Hackney Half
arathons, London Landmarks Half
arathon, The Big Half, trail running, trail
n festivals and have even had one
ember do the holy grail, The London
arathon, with Coffee Runners cheering
r the whole way. And many more socials
d events to boot.

he main group is the original Hackney
e, but we have had community funded
oups and ventures in Tower Hamlets
ith a group in partnership with
Margaret's House, using Mile End
rkrun as our finish.

WHAT HAPPENS IF IT RAINS?

I believe in the benefits of being outdoors.
One of the things I always get asked when
people start is "What happens if it rains?"
My reply "We get wet." My role as coach
is to remind people that they can do it
whatever the weather, even snow, to
encourage and motivate whilst fostering
a supportive and competitive atmosphere
in the group. Nothing makes me happier
when I'm out in the neighbourhood and
I spot a Coffee Runner, past or present,
out running by themselves.

Photo courtesy Gigi Giannella

MOM SPED TO THE FINISH

DIANA VALK

My first memories of running are not of me running, but of my mom. She would come into the house dripping with sweat, her pale Northumbrian complexion briefly transformed to a scarlet colour after running in the heat of the sweltering Georgia summer. This was a common occurrence in our house because running was a need for my mom, almost as necessary as water, air and food.

Most weekends my family would pile into the car and go to whatever race happened to be on – The Dog Days 5 miler, The Run Around the Rock, The Maggie Valley Moonlight Run. Sometimes I would participate in the associated children's fun run, but often I'd just watch proudly as my mom sped to the finish, winning her age group or even the overall female masters award. Seeing this happen so frequently gave me the impression that lots of women ran and that it was commonplace to come home with an award after every race. It's only age and my own running experiences that have shown me how far from normal both these things were at the time.

When I got older I asked my mom how it was being a female runner in the 1960s and 70s. She would tell stories of people hurling insults at her from passing cars, yelling lewd remarks as she ran through the neighbourhoods, or even obstructing her path as she attempted to do speedwork on the track. Once a police officer stopped her and asked her what she was running from – that's how uncommon it was for people to see a woman out running.

Although I didn't grow up feeling the compulsion to run like my mom, I now find it an integral part of my life. I'm definitely not raking in the medals like her, but that' not why I run, and it was never why she ran. Instead, I find it necessary for my mental wellbeing. Not only does it help me manage the small hurdles of everyday life but it has also allowed me to weather more substantial problems. When a major relationship ended, I threw myself into training for my first half marathon. When I was lonely and depressed, working for long stretches away from home, I would turn to running to lift my spirits. Even during the Covid lockdown running has given me something to look forward to during the day.

When I return to the US to visit my family, I often go to the track with my mom. Injury prevents her from running, but she will walk while I do my intervals and afterwards we'll talk life and running. Like me, she considers running, and exercise in general, a cure all for her stresses. If not for the emotional support running gave her, she doesn't know where she'd be. Her speed might not have made it into my genes, but her love and need of running certainly did.

MR OVARY
CRAIG McMURROUGH

Sadly and tragically in 2016 I lost my sister to ovarian cancer. Since then I have been running as Mr Ovary. I normally run the London Marathon in a six-foot Giant Ovary to raise awareness and raise funds for ovarian cancer charity Ovacome. I often team up with my buddy Graham who sings karaoke as he runs and we call ourselves Karaoke Ovary – it's a fab way to entertain the crowds and runners at the big events like the Great North Run and London Marathon. We collect a lot of cash on the day as well – I carry the buckets!

A PROLIFIC FUNDRAISER

I am a prolific fundraiser having raised over £50,000 for Ovacome and competing in 19 marathons. I also completed a climb of Mount Kilimanjaro and placed a photo of my sister Cheryl and an Ovacome T-shirt at the summit.

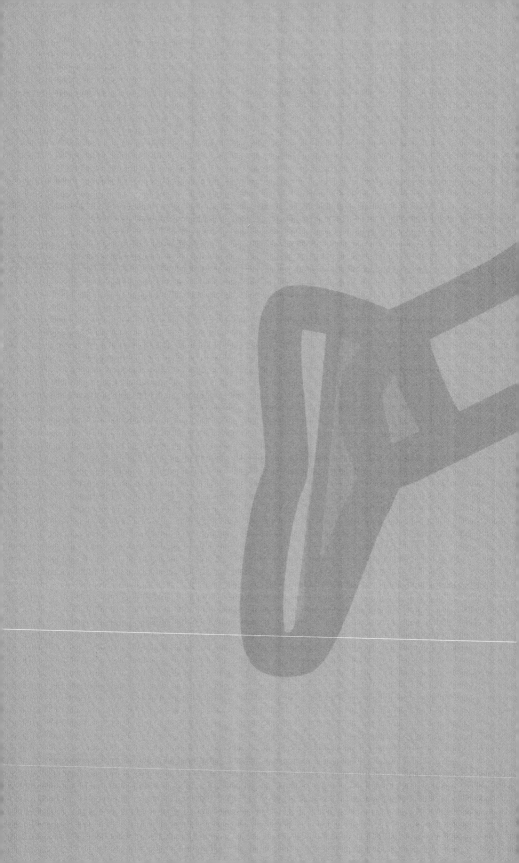

IT MAKES ME FEEL SO GOOD

I RUN FOR JOY
MALCOLM BERESFORD

I run to be free, to live, to discover, to experience and enjoy. I run for the countryside, the flower-scented air, the moor and the forest. I run for the lochs, the streams, and the bog, and the dark, dank places, where the mini beasts live and play.

I run for Nature in all Her moods, numbing cold of winter, burning glare of summer sun. Balmy late summer evenings and bracing spring mornings.

I run for the honey sweet singing at dawn, and the timid little fawn I met, deep in the forest. I run for the pets and pests, the welcome and not. The innocent youngster, and the wise old soul, the yapping puppy and the steady old stager. For those finding out, and those who have found. And those who will not find... those who know not how to look.

I RUN SO YOU MAY KNOW ME, MY MASK REMOVED

I run for your blessing, affection and love, the endless embrace and your always warm heart. I run for your joy, admiration, and pride, seeing me spent in the delirium of effort and exhaustion. I run so you may know me, my mask removed, no social niceties, just dried off sweat, and poorly concealed tears. I run for you and with you, behind and in front, seen and unseen. We venture life's short trail together and not, alone and apart, smiling, crying, laughing, dying.

I run to know the joy of challenge, of effort, of work. The honesty of Man and Nature, respect for the known, search for the unknown. I run for the life of endeavour, the steepest hill, and the rockiest track, the greatest distance, and the tingling adventure of deepest darkness.

And cruel lost love, distant love and love that never was, but could have been, and should have been. Regrets and mistakes, lovers passed by, love that was there, but unseen and unknown.

I RUN FOR LIFE TO ENJOY EVERY MOMENT

I run for self-knowledge, without which we know no others. I run for joy, to give and to share. I run for life, to enjoy every moment.

This run may be our last, go on with a smile, and return with a laugh, avoiding Old Nick once more.

IT'S JUST ME
ANDY WALL

The reason I run is pretty simple – because I can. I do lots of sports and spend lots of time outside and moving. I have a big, strong body and I like to see where my limits are. I don't mind a bit of pain, and running has taught me to work through pain, to rename it and turn it into something useful.

RUNNING TEACHES ME WHAT I'M MADE OF

Running makes me proud of my strength and perseverance and humbled by the weakness of my flesh and my thoughts. Running teaches me what I'm made of and gives me an idea of who I could be. When I run all day, I am broken down and built back up, and turned into someone new.

WHEN I'M RUNNING IT'S JUST ME. IT'S MY CHOICE

In other sports I always have a piece of equipment or a refinement to my technique that can give me an assist or magnify my power or speed. When I'm running, it's just me. It's my choice.

RUNNING EMPOWERS ME
RAHEMA MAMODO

Running was something I never previously enjoyed; in fact, I had never considered it to be something someone like me would ever do. My childhood consisted of little to no physical activity and I was never encouraged to do so. This continued throughout most of my life and as I grew up, my level of activeness continued to decrease. After years of being inactive, I finally decided it was time for a change and took the opportunity to join a local Couch to 5k running group in November 2018. This was my chance to get more active and hopefully to inspire my three daughters. Being something completely foreign to me, I was very apprehensive to join. However, I managed to rope in a good friend to join me, making it more fun and less likely for me to back out.

MY FIRST TIME RUNNING OUTSIDE IN PUBLIC

I had no clue what I was about to face. Anxiety filled my head in the days leading up to the first session. This was going to be my first time running outside in public and just the thought of that alone was unsettling. Not to mention the fact that my head scarf made me feel even more self-conscious. I had many thoughts running through my mind, the most intimidating being the judgment of passers-by or drivers.

At first, I decided to sign up for just the one week, this was going to be a trial session for me. I was hesitant to commit more than

that in case my performance was very poor. Contrary to my initial uneasy thoughts, I was given peace of mind almost immediately by the run leader and fellow runners. I came out of the first session feeling relieved and euphoric as to what I had just achieved. I felt even more proud that I did not back out, despite the weather being cold and wet. Furthermore, I was surprised that I felt the urge to go back the following week!

I WAS ATTRACTED TO THE FRIENDLY ATMOSPHERE AND COMMOTION

The first 5k run I completed was also my first parkrun, which I really enjoyed. I was attracted to the friendly atmosphere and commotion, as well as the inclusivity. That first 5k was a challenge for me but it was an achievement, one I never thought I would accomplish. It felt even better that I was able to do it with my friend. From that day I was captivated and made the decision to attend the local parkrun weekly. To my surprise, as I continued to attend, I became confident enough to go on my own every week. In addition to doing the parkrun, I pushed myself to start running more often during the week. This was a struggle at first, and I found it hard to step out of my own front door. The lack of confidence and fear of being judged was something that I had to work on and continue to do so to this day.

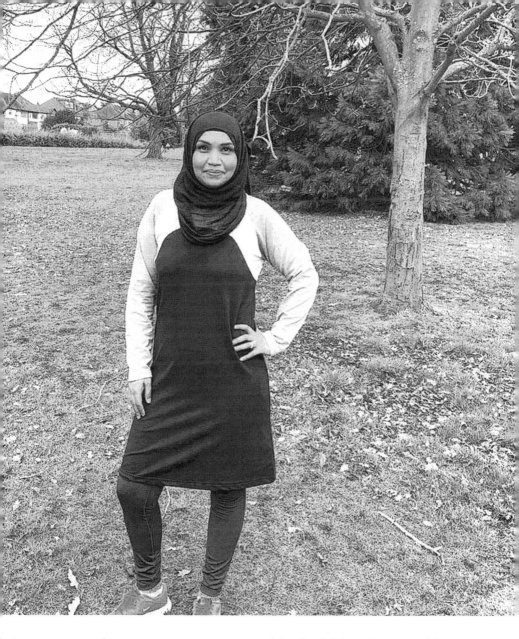

RUNNERS COME IN ALL SHAPES AND SIZES

Running empowers me. It improves my mental health, clears my mind, and allows me to be proud of myself as an inspiration towards my children. I have since run two half marathons, one of which was within a year of the first Couch to 5k session, something that I did not deem possible. But it was this that fuelled my confidence to continue running and one day I wish to complete a full marathon. I may not be the fastest runner out there and judging by my appearance you probably wouldn't think I am a runner, but runners come in all shapes and sizes and from all kinds of backgrounds.

THE MOUNTAINS ARE CALLING
FIONA ENGLISH

I have no desire to win races. For many, times, medals, Instagramable pictures and being competitive is a huge driver to participating in sport. But it just isn't for me.

I was once told by an incredible ultramarathon runner I know, that if you don't stand on the starting line of a race not knowing if you can finish it or not, it isn't a challenge. Not because you haven't trained hard enough, or put in the work, or aren't healthy but because exploring your own boundaries of possibility and limits is where we discover who we really are.

When I first took up running, I remember finding the idea of running for a kilometre without stopping mind blowing. Now I feel confident running for about eight hours without needing to walk. As I've tested my own boundaries and limits, I've been consistently shocked by just how much further and faster and higher I can go. Months of training, hard work and a huge amount of dogged determination has seen me complete marathons, ultras, mountain races and even Ironman.

MY ENTHUSIASM IS MY DESIRE TO PURSUE ADVENTURE

Along the way, I've realised that I have no desire to stick at one thing and 'be the best'. My enthusiasm is my desire to pursue adventure. Relentlessly. With abandon. Passionately. Adventure is calling.

Don't get me wrong: PBs are amazing. For me personally as a coach, there are two things that are particularly joyous to watch: new runners shocked at achieving things they never thought possible, and runners who'd counted themselves out for a long time and suddenly surprise themselves. I've been through both of those. I've cried my eyes out at finish lines for achieving times that seemed 'too fast' for the runner I assumed I was. And yet when I look back at my favourite memories in running, numbers don't feature.

THERE WAS THE TIME I PACED MY MUM

There is the moment in my Ironman where I crossed paths with my husband, an hour up the race from me, and we shared a kiss before finishing our respective marathons. There was the time I paced my Mum, who'd promised me she'd never do any sport in her life, to complete her first 10k at the age of 70. There are the miles and miles I've spent traipsing up and down some remote mountain in Scotland with my Dad talking about anything and everything.

Fear of missing out and defining yourself by others' achievements is a dangerous and unsatisfying pathway. What if we all put aside the relentless marathon cycles and 5k PB hunts and just pursued adventure? Maybe we'd miss our time goals and what our peers might consider

ood' times, but instead we might nd something our hearts had been earning for.

hn Muir, one of the great advocates for e power of the outdoors in the late ineteenth century, famously said: he mountains are calling and I must go." feel that call. Trapped in our city lives surrounded by constant noise and busyness and progress, it's easy to feel the overwhelming rise of fear and anxiety that grips so many of us. When I am in nature, I truly feel I am in a space where I remember what matters: not my job title, PBs, finishing position in some random half marathon, but connection, love, passion, joy.

NOTHING STOPS ME
ANNIE TRIHAN

I am from Moscow, Russia originally – but grew up in Idaho and Oregon, USA from age 10.

I LIKE EVERYTHING ABOUT RUNNING AND HOW IT MAKES ME FEEL

I started running during my senior year of high school, to stay in shape for my first love, tennis. I remember running my first mile and throwing up afterwards (and let's be clear, not only was I not fast, I was literally the last one done). I like everything about running and how it makes me feel. I like doing it in my own time and being alone, and I like running with my club or as part of parkrun.

When I travel, I love waking up early exploring new places on foot, finding my bearings, and seeing things I wouldn't have otherwise seen.

I like the runs that feel easy and you're not looking at your watch, and the ones that feel hard where you only like them when you're done!

I like the structure of training and the sense of accomplishment that comes with pushing through new barriers as a result of diligent work. And I like how I feel when I am fit – strong and powerful.

My biggest motivation is to run happy, and to give it my best. Nothing really stops me – I have to be pretty ill or busy not to run.

I used to listen to music but not anymore. I like to hear what's going on around me, it adds to my experience. I look and listen to what is around me if I'm somewhere new. If it's my same old routes, I focus on breathing, trying to guess if I will see anyone I know running, or see how close I can get to guessing exactly where the km markers are.

Photo courtesy Gigi Giannella

IT MAKES ME FEEL SO GOOD

WORTH THE EFFORT
OLIVIA KILMARTIN

I only started running last year – at the young age of 65. It was a spur of the moment thing. I saw a flyer for a running club when I was bored queueing at the post office and thought I would go along and see what it was like.

I WAS SO SURPRISED HOW MUCH I ENJOYED IT

It was one of the best decisions of my life – I was so surprised how much I enjoyed it. I had no idea what 'Couch to 5k' meant. When I realised the sessions were designed with the goal of running five kilometres at the end of the term, I was very doubtful I was up to it, and frankly nervous at the idea. But I did it and I haven't looked back. One of the satisfying things is I am fitter in my sixties than I ever was. Just goes to show it's never too late.

Running is a challenge sometimes – I often feel reluctant to go running in the mornings thinking I am too tired, too hung-over, have too many other things to do, but once I'm out there with the others, running in the open air, I find it lifts my mood every time. I even enjoy running in the rain. I've yet to do it in the snow, but I'm sure one day I will.

I was laughed at by my fellow runners – in a very friendly way I hasten to add – for my running clothes. I wear anything running, but I am proud of my bright orange Coffee Run T-shirt and my London Relay T-shirt that I was given for taking

Photo courtesy Gigi Giannella

part in the 10k London Relay. And I was persuaded to spend a lot of money on proper running shoes.

I tried listening to the radio while running but found it distracting. I prefer to run with others and chat if we're not too puffed out!

I AM AN ADDICT
CAROLINE GILBY

Hello, my name is Caroline and I am an addict.

THERE ARE MANY WORSE ADDICTIONS I COULD HAVE

I haven't run for 72 hours. I feel weirdly twitchy and have been snapping at the family for no reason – proper withdrawal symptoms. I am happy to admit that I'm a running addict. After all, there are many worse addictions I could have.

I've been running on and off since cross-country at school, when a friend and I worked out that if we ran fast, we could go home early. At university, I took up Modern Pentathlon which suited me fine as it allowed me to be vaguely competent at five sports rather than excelling at any of them. And running was one of those sports (along with fencing, swimming, shooting and horse riding). Eventually having to work for a living took over and sport disappeared out of my life for quite a few years, except a bit of target shooting, and that doesn't require much fitness.

I only started running regularly as a proper grown-up when I went on a study trip to New Zealand back in 1993. I work with wine (back then as a buyer, nowadays as a writer) and wine producers tend to be incredibly generous and hospitable, always keen to show off their wines with the best food. Hotel breakfasts, followed by multiple gourmet courses for lunch, dinner and mid-afternoon snacks looked set to destroy my waistline unless I did

something, so I started running, and never really looked back.

I carried on pottering for years, just really jogging to keep my job at bay, until one day in 2001, I thought I might have a go at a Race for Life (somewhat ironic looking back that my first ever running race was in aid of Cancer Research). I honestly didn't have any idea that I had any speed in my legs so was totally flabbergasted to finish in the top dozen. Up till then I had assumed running clubs were for serious athletes only and that I would be way too slow to keep up. One Sunday morning not long after, I plucked up courage to turn up at my local running club, and it turned out to be a group of mostly normal human beings of all shapes, sizes and speeds, some of whom have become very dear friends.

TOTALLY FLABBERGASTED TO FINISH IN THE TOP DOZEN

Nowadays running is an essential part of my life for so many reasons. It helps keep the crappy side effects of my various cancer drugs at bay (these include weight gain, bone loss and lowered cardiovascular health) and it gives me the feeling that I am doing something positive to help myself, rather than just letting treatment happen to me. And it seems there is some evidence that exercise is a good thing, both in helping to lower your cancer risk (yeah right, that bit worked so well for me) and improving chances of survival.

IT MAKES ME FEEL SO GOOD

148

Photo courtesy David JW Bailey

GOING FOR A RUN OFTEN HELPS ME WITH WORK

Running also helps me in other ways: it pushes the circling black dogs away to a safe distance, and it provides me with me-time when I can run away from my woes, leaving them behind as I shut the front door. Going for a run often helps me with work – writer's block is an inevitability in my job, but I frequently find the right words pop into my head during a run (and yes I have been known to phone home and leave a message with said words in case I forget).

Running is also often a social thing for me. I have several good friends that I run with, putting the world to rights as we explore the countryside (if we can't talk and run, we are going too fast). Friends who have really been there for me through the bad times too.

And those withdrawal symptoms – easily dealt with by a nice hill session in the local woods.

I'M UNSTOPPABLE
SARAH WATSON

I started running at Easter 2017. A group of us were in the pub and one, Lucy, asked who wanted to help her train for a 10k run. I said "I don't even run for buses." Overnight, I thought about that and realised I was closing off possibilities, rather than trying something new. I didn't have a good reason not to take part. And I got FOMO (Fear of Missing Out). I thought the others might end up having fun without me. So, I went along to their first training session the next day.

I run for fitness and for fun. Working from home it's important to make an effort to get up and out. It's sociable and it's been amazing over the last three and a half years to discover more of what I can do. In this photo I'm on a corner of two paths in the park where we trained to start with. Getting to this corner felt like such an achievement in the early days: "let's make it to the corner then have a rest." It's nice to look back and see the journey.

Today I ran for 30 minutes. For my first Half Marathon in 2018 I loved working towards something that I had previously considered far beyond my capability, it was really motivating. So is going for a PB at parkrun – looking at the stats afterwards and seeing how you and your buddies did that day is really great. Having a fixed appointment to run with someone else is very helpful – it means that the runs actually happen and keeps me going when I might stop if I were alone.

What stops me? I've re-written this six times debating whether or not to say it, but hey, it's important and I should make no apology for this – period pain knocks me right off kilter and it shouldn't be taboo to admit it. When my insides are feeling kicked in, running efficiently and comfortably doesn't happen. Other than these things?! – I'm unstoppable! (I wish...)

I run alongside other people usually, so I don't listen to music. And I like to say hello to people, especially other runners – my way of encouraging community spirit in London.

Photo courtesy Gigi Giannella

IT MAKES ME FEEL SO GOOD

RUNNING KEPT ME SANE
ATSUKO WHITEHOUSE

Every morning I run unless it is raining heavily. Get up, look outside to see the weather, change into my running gear, go downstairs and sip hot water with a slice of lemon just before opening the front door. It is almost a ritual ceremony.

Fresh cold air on my skin is a wonderful feeling. If I can see the sunrise during my morning run, my day is almost perfect.

I am Japanese. I came to London 27 years ago when I married my husband, who is British. We have two grown up children.

COMPLETED A 100K, VERY SLOWLY, LAST YEAR

I started to run to get fit. I ran my first marathon when I was almost 50 and ran more marathons before I completed 100K, very slowly, last year.

IT GROUNDS ME, MAKES MY HEAD CLEAR

I love to set a target and achieve it, but running is not just that. It grounds me, makes my head clear and helps me prioritise what is important.

Life is tough sometimes; losing my brother then my father soon after, and leaving my mother alone in Japan, were not easy. Running has kept me sane throughout and I am sure it will continue to do so.

I AM FREE
LIZZIE CURRIE

Emil Zátopek, the legendary long-distance runner, famously said "If you want to win something run 100m, if you want to experience something run a marathon."

IT'S MY HAPPY PILL, MY THERAPY, MY SPACE, AND MY TIME

Running came into my life late, after the birth of my third child, and has been so important. It's my happy pill, my therapy, my space, and my time. When I was younger it was an avenue for my competitive spirit, racing, beating PBs, striving to go faster and better, but as I have got older I have learnt to adapt, to run further and for longer, and it has become more about the journey and about the wonderful parts of the world I can explore through running. I have been lucky enough to run through mountains, across deserts, along coastlines and through many beautiful cites in the world.

I RUN TO SHOW MY CHILDREN WITHOUT WORDS THAT I VALUE MYSELF

People often ask me why I run. I run to show my children without words that I value myself, my mental health, my physical body, my fitness, and my time. It helps me show them that I need balance in my life, just as they do in theirs. They see me train long and train hard, they watch me push myself, they see me make

Photo courtesy iancorless.com

sacrifices, endure injury and pain and best of all they see me succeed and deal with disappointment, and that it's OK to fail, it's how we learn and grow and get

IT MAKES ME FEEL SO GOOD

152

tronger. They watch as I pick myself up,
y another way, find another adventure,
ot dwell on the things I can no longer do
s I get older, but celebrate new journeys
that lie ahead. Hopefully, some of this will
be useful as they prepare for the races they
will face in their own lives.

SCRATCHING THE SURFACE

CLYDE WILLIAMSON

JANUARY

After a chilly run, I noticed somewhere between 15-20 small red dots located below my armpit, on the sides of my stomach.

These 'dots' stood out significantly and resembled chickenpox, without the itchiness.

I am currently studying for my four-year BA Hons degree at Duncan of Jordanstone, University of Dundee. Shortly after returning to Uni from Christmas I made a lunchtime trip to the campus GP. I had psoriasis. This didn't really worry me because it's not dangerous, it's not life-threatening, you can manage it, but you can't cure it. Although this auto-immune condition doesn't harm your life, it will make it uncomfortable and less enjoyable. I didn't know this yet, and I rambled on running with positivity, consistency and unfortunately, naivety.

FEBRUARY

I spent some wonderful, soaking, and snowy days running through the glens around the Glenfinnan area, sometimes slipping to my waist in deceptively gushing streams, masked by wild and relentless heather. This entire area was uncharted for me and I will never forget the cold and damp night spent in Pean Bothy.

During my last day in Glenfinnan I ran a euphoria-filled high-level round of some of the Munros, easily accessed from the single-track road leading through the glen. I set off up the road in thick cloud, eventually burning through the final layer halfway up the first climb. I was almost instantly consumed within glorious morning beams and views of Ben Nevis, the Cuillin Ridge and the all-too-familiar Pean Bothy far below – which appeared picturesque before uninterrupted early-blue skies.

I spent that night in my Grandma's house in Banavie, where I ate third helpings and two desserts (her idea). We spoke of the going-ons in the town until we were both too tired. I also had one of the best showers and the best sleeps I have ever had. I slept peacefully, enjoying the simple pleasures I had come to miss, concealing memories of unimaginable value. I am forever grateful for the way she took me in, never once questioning why I had just slept in the family car for a week. By the morning, my wet sleeping bag she had hung by the fire was completely dry.

MARCH

The university was closed due to Covid-19. By then my psoriasis covered my entire upper body, my hips, my rear-end, my face, my neck, and my arms. Running was reduced to almost zero, as sometimes just walking or bending over was a painful ordeal. I was not too chuffed about that. Since starting uni I have joined both the rucksack club for mountaineering trips and the athletics club, where we train twice a week and compete in road, cross-country and hill races. Within this club I have made fantastic friendships and found opportunities to venture my running into

suspicious with a buff, sunglasses, and a baseball cap. In the strangest ways, it was all quite good timing. By this time all my close friends had left. I was starting to feel quite alone. Additionally, my legs looked like swollen, bloody tree trunks.

JUNE

I have started running again. Since escaping back home to Aberdeenshire and making the right changes, I am starting to heal. I have changed my diet, enjoyed ample sunlight, and made an ointment from Comfrey suggested by a friend. It's been a rocky six months, and for a long time I ignored the signs of illness, did all the wrong things, and ran too hard. What I do know is that running, although I was not physically doing it, is what kept my mind alive during particularly difficult times, whilst the condition was at its worst.

Psoriasis has changed me in some ways. It has made me appreciate the real things that build a person's spirit throughout their life, and the communities of supportive relationships we create through a shared and simple passion for moving fast. As runners, we are translating the bare-naked essence of our being into the physical state of working towards our goals. Running is a development not only of your muscles and your organs, but also of your mind, your perspective, your adaptability and your presence – alongside close people, with whom we share a lifetime of memories, formed in the depths and the heights of sweat and happiness.

completely new competitions and disciplines that I had never considered before. I was running seven days a week – twice on training days. I was racing the best I had ever raced. However, this all came to a very sudden stop.

APRIL-MAY

The days of 'mild' psoriasis were gone. It was becoming 'severe'. The large, dry, itchy, red, and flaking patches of damaged skin covered everything, from head to toe. Any mobility or flexing of my arms and legs was incredibly agonising. My face looked like I had been in an awful fight, and very sunburnt. I slowly became more embarrassed about my appearance in public. Luckily, everyone in Tesco had their faces covered so I didn't always look

I NEED TO RUN
ADRIAN LOBB

Madonna had it right. "Only when I'm dancing can I feel this free," she sang on Into The Groove. These words summed up my 20s and early 30s.

I HAD STOPPED RUNNING WHEN I WAS 15

This was my running interregnum. I had stopped running when I was 15. At school, I ran the 1500m and the occasional cross country. I never won races, but I tried hard, thought about tactics, watched the greats of a golden era – Steve Ovett, Steve Cram, Sebastian Coe, Liz McColgan and Zola Budd.

Sixth form college meant no track and field, no cross country, no running – a relief for many young people, no doubt. And I didn't mind too much. There was always football, for a couple of years.

THEN THERE WAS DANCING

And then? Then there was dancing. A lot of dancing. Nightclubs galore. Every night a different dancefloor. The blessed solitude of immersing myself in song, dancing alone together – alongside and surrounded by other people, but mostly in my own interior world. Dancing. Feeling free.

We didn't talk about our mental health then. But if we had and I'd had any sense of self-analysis, I'd have pinpointed my dancing feet as the tools I used to protect my head. Cut to my mid-30s, with my dancing days fading despite my best intentions. Suddenly, there was running

again. A faithful, forgotten friend. Ready to pick me up where we had left off.

I SAW ALL THE RUNNERS STREAMING ACROSS THE TYNE BRIDGE

I was inspired to run again by watching The Great North Run, looking for one face in the crowd – the same face I'd first seen in a Soho Nightclub 12 years earlier. From the train, on my way to watch the finish of the race, I saw all the runners streaming across the Tyne Bridge. Not an inch of tarmac in view, just thousands of runners. What a sight to behold, what a thing to be part of – what a feeling of jealousy and longing it stirred up. I vowed to run it next year. And have been running it ever since.

I could still run. That was a relief. I was now a bit taller and, at first, a bit slower. Finding the motivation was difficult, especially to run on my own. Self-motivation is tough to cultivate.

But alongside finding a stillness through the perpetual movement, running gradually reignited a competitive edge I'd not had for decades – less serious and earnest now, less obsessed than I was as a teenager. But a desire to improve, that feeling of racing to beat both my previous best times and the person in front, even if they didn't know we were racing.

Sometimes I still have to remind myself to enjoy it. The open air. The quiet roads. The parks. The solitude. The pure freedom

f putting one foot in front of another, while allowing one thought to follow another. Sometimes I'm thinking about running too much instead of looking at the concrete dinosaurs in my local park or enjoying the trees and dogs and people during training runs.

On race days or parkrun Saturdays, there is – that old dancefloor feeling. Alone in crowd, dancing to your own tune,

running your own race, part of something, belonging to a big, warm, sweaty community. And it is intoxicating.

I STILL LOVE TO DANCE

I still love to dance. But I need to run. Only when I'm running can I feel this free.

Adrian is a Trustee of The Running Charity.

MY TIMES ARE MY OWN
DARREN EVANS

I ran as a child and ran through my teens
I ran through my 20s, trying out for the Marines
Then kids came along, and time disappeared
No time for running as children were reared
Working all hours through 30s and 40s
Time flying by, especially the 'noughties'
Then when I was 50, I injured my spine
Came off my bike, recovery fine
But needed more fitness, after recovery phase
So, got out my trainers and jogged a few days
Started to get faster, felt better inside
Was enjoying my running and running with pride
Entered some races, 10k and a half
How about a marathon, "you're having a laugh!"
I love rural running, the hills and the trails
Sunny or rainy, the wind and the hails
I prefer solo running, no music in ears
Just listening to nature, I lose all my fears
This is my headspace, my answer to stress
I run for myself and not to impress
My times are my own, we all run our races
Some need motivation to pick up their paces
I just need some trainers, a trail and a phone
Within 15 minutes I am into the zone
My breathing in rhythm, feet fly on the ground
A passion for running again I have found

IT MAKES ME FEEL SO GOOD

I AM FREE
JAN SMITH

I've been running for just over 15 years now, and my motivation to do it over this time has varied greatly. Initially, it was to keep me from smoking, and it moved to training for events, losing weight (after Christmas and babies!) and maintaining my health.

My job involves 'holding' other people's pain and suffering. It can feel pretty intense at times. I've never really thought about why I run, I just do. However, about a year ago someone asked me, did I ever feel I was running from something when I ran? I laughed, thinking what a strange question, but it sparked a curiosity in me, a questioning of sorts.

WHEN I RUN NOTHING IS EXPECTED OF ME, DEMANDED FROM ME

Why did I run? For me, it's not that I'm running from something, rather I'm running towards something. When I run, nothing is expected from me, demanded from me. I don't have to think, feel or be all the roles that I am. Instead I am 'held', in nature. I am free!

IT MAKES ME FEEL SO GOOD

TIME UNFIXED
JOE ANTHONY

used to run on my toes
With my allotted time
The point was feeling and being over
he cigarettes

nd alcohol

Now I run with a midfoot strike
Time unfixed
I splay my fingers
Find a line
And sometimes all is well with the world

I USED TO RUN ON MY TOES
WITH MY ALLOTTED TIME

THE DREAM
JOSE SANCHEZ ALONSO-MARDONES

I started running in 2014 to follow my wife, she was always looking great after a run, so I gave it a try. Sadly, I didn't get the same high, however it helped me to reduce the extra kilograms I was gaining (damn you cheap cheesecakes!).

After five years I'm loving running a bit more every day, the challenges, the little improvements, the shock in the people from my past when I tell them that I am a runner (priceless).

YOU MAY BE HEARING ME ON PARKRUNS BREATHING LIKE AN OLD LOCOMOTIVE TRAIN!

I really enjoy running as fast as I can and giving it all. You may be hearing me on parkruns breathing like an old locomotive train!

Long runs are still tough, I did my first marathon two years ago (ending with five kilometres of agony), and still with some self-doubts I will try it again this November.

Probably ageing is getting me motivated, with 37 years on my back and getting closer to the 40s barrier, running can be a lifesaver. I have never felt fitter, and if I can still run in my 50s, who knows, maybe I will win races in my age category (what a dream).

IT MAKES ME FEEL SO GOOD

Photo courtesy Gigi Giannella

DOG SPIRIT
KATSURA ISOBE

I am Katsura, originally from Tokyo, I have been settled in London for a long time.

I have always been active since a young age but have never been a committed runner. I started running more regularly, once or twice a week, about five years ago.

WITHOUT RUNNING, I COULD FEEL VERY LOW

Today I've run 8.5km. I run to keep fit. I also realised that running boosts my mood. Without running, I could feel very low. I especially enjoy running outdoors, feeling the breeze and light, noticing nature changing with the seasons, listening to birds singing, and passing dog walkers. Then sometimes a surge of joy and freedom comes up. I feel I am just part of the whole landscape, nothing different from that dog rolling on the grass.

When I feel tired and want to be lazy it is a challenge to get motivated for a run. Then I really have to tell myself to leave the concrete box and take back the dog spirit.

I never listen to music while running. A dog would not need to listen to music to run, would she?

Photo courtesy Gigi Giannella

I WAS HOOKED
MIRY MAYER

I'm Miry, I was born in Russia and made London my home 15 years ago.

Until six years ago, running was more like an awful chore, something to avoid. I'd look at runners' facial expressions and all I'd see was suffering I had no intention of putting myself through.

One day at the gym, while doing fast incline walking I noticed that although the person on the treadmill next to mine wasn't built like the typical skinny runner, he kept an impressive and consistent pace.

A competitive button was pressed and next time at the gym I decided to try running instead of walking. I lasted barely three and a half minutes, earning myself a massive slice of humble pie. But I tried again and again, until I could run for 30 minutes without stopping. And when I finally decided to brave the outdoors, watching my familiar surroundings whoosh past me by the power of my legs and lungs – I was hooked.

IT MAKES ME FEEL SO GOOD

Photo courtesy Gigi Giannella

IT'S THE PSYCHOLOGICAL AND SPIRITUAL LIFTS THAT I ENJOY MOST

I normally run four times a week, and while the physical benefits are the most obvious, it's the psychological and spiritual lifts that I enjoy the most. This is the time I switch off from the daily grind, exploring the world around me and finding hidden fragments of beauty, creating moments of joy. It's a challenge fitting my runs into my busy life, but the feeling of accomplishment that I get from overcoming tiredness, busy schedules, and general laziness, extends to other areas of my life. Every new thing starts with a first step, and I've proved to myself over and over again that I am capable of taking that step.

I'm wearing a T-shirt with a running bear wearing trainers. Apart from the Russian connection, bears are incredible endurance runners, challenging the perception that you need a gazelle-like build to be an accomplished runner.

DO WHAT FEELS GOOD

LILY LANG

Although this story has a happy ending, my relationship with running (and exercise in general) started a little more problematic than I realised at the time. I was heavily steeped in disordered eating and used running to control my weight and burn as many calories as possible. I ended up with knee problems, shin splints, the works! I didn't really enjoy running or exercise but convinced myself I did because of my lifelong commitment to being thin.

When I ran, I ran on the treadmill. I would count down the minutes until I got off and stared at the calories being burned as if I was watching a thrilling soap opera. Nevertheless, I signed for the Barcelona Marathon 2017 and soon realised that I could not run more than 5k on a treadmill and needed some outdoor stimulation. I downloaded an app to track my mileage and started running outside, and suddenly began to genuinely, really, love it.

I gained a real sense of freedom when running outdoors and the scenery in parks or even sometimes roads really calmed my mind. I found that when I ran, the nagging voices which told me I wasn't good enough, the anxiety about whether I had left the kitchen tap on, and the general stress from the day soon lifted. Most importantly, as soon as I saw my mileage increase, I felt a sense of pride in what my body could do. This led me to start feeding myself a more adequate amount of food.

My experience with running hasn't always

been easy. I love running and I now run for my mental health, a love of the outdoors and to relieve stress or anxiety, but I've overdone it many times. I've beat myself up for taking a day off, running to the point of exhaustion and injury. We live in a culture that idolises 'health', 'fitness' and 'thinness' and it's really important to try to find a balance that is right for you and to recognise that being thin or running 10k do not equate to perfect health. Find some movement you enjoy and remember it is not about having to burn off every calorie that you eat. Far from it. It's about having the freedom and the permission to move your body in a way that feels good for you, whatever your size or shape. If that's running, then that's great, but if you prefer walking, lifting, or doing a seated meditation then that is equally valid.

I still run frequently, but I take days or weeks off if I feel I need to. The best lesson I have learned about exercise is that sometimes, not doing it is just as beneficial for your body as doing it. Listen to your body and do what feels good.

WAITING TO GET ADDICTED
KITTY STEWART

I'm Kitty. I'm a Londoner.

Really, I run because it takes less time than going swimming, which I'm much better at.

And if I'm working at home it's great to get out in the morning and see the trees and the sky (sometimes even the sun), especially in winter.

Plus, it's always nice to have a chat with the lovely Coffee Runners, and it's great feeling fit enough to run for the bus.

I STILL HAVEN'T GOT TO THE POINT WHERE I LOVE THE ACTUAL RUNNING PART

But I must admit I still haven't got to the point where I love the actual running part. I'm waiting patiently to get addicted, like everyone says happens, but it's been a few years now and I'm not quite there yet!

IT MAKES ME FEEL SO GOOD

Photo courtesy Gigi Giannella

166

FASTER THAN THE BOYS
NIKKI LAKIN

I am Nikki, and have been in Hackney for 7 years, formerly of Hertfordshire via Gloucestershire. At eight or nine years old I discovered I could run faster than all the boys in my year – so I did, as often as I could. Until my teenage pride told me it was 'uncool'. I came back to it in my 20s but am way stronger now in my 40s – ever since having kids I've realised that anything is easy compared to giving birth.

I run for brain space. To feel the simplicity of 'it's just me'. It's meditation – clears my head and reminds me that I'm powerful and capable (even through the tribulations of my six and eight-year-old kids).

I'm motivated to get into the (sometimes) fresh air, see the trees, feel the elements, and watch the seasons change. I've been running long enough that the challenge comes when I don't. It's a habit – a fact that understates how grateful I am I can do it.

Autumn chill is in the air, so the long leggings are out – plus a base layer and my club T-shirt (another challenge of running: no one yet makes the perfect lightweight rain-proof jacket!). Coffee Run Hackney is just a bunch of local people who run and try to get fitter together – no stress, no expectations – a mutual cheer squad. For years I was a solo runner but joining is the best thing I've done – for my running and for my social life. Sometimes we go for coffee, and sometimes we go... do a 10k in Geneva, or trail-running in Wales, or wild swimming in Stoke Newington... it's varied, and a great laugh.

Photo courtesy Gigi Giannella

TWO CONTRASTING VIEWS

I HATE RUNNING
DR JOHN ETHERINGTON

I hate running
Particularly in the morning
With boots on
In the rain
Carrying heavy equipment
And a weapon
But generally – I hate running

John spent 35 years in the Army where all physical activity was running.

ENERGY
AOIRSE SMITH

I like running ~~because~~ it gives me a lot of ~~energe~~ energy.

Saoirse Smith

6

THE RUNNING CHARITY

The Running Charity delivers running and personal development programmes to young people aged 16-25 who are affected by homelessness. We are a small charity formed in 2014 in London, now also active in Manchester, Leeds and Brighton, with plans to expand to other areas.

Our programme of active wellbeing supports young people through some of life's most challenging obstacles, providing community, key work support, access to therapy, and personal development coaching. All these interactions are aimed at enhancing an individual's toolkit to cope better with the immense adversities they face.

We help young people who have had difficult pasts to get back on their feet, using a goal setting and reward system to develop the habit of achieving. By using running to start and maintain long-term relationships, we enable them to make positive decisions about the direction of their future.

We are proud that on joining us, young people who consistently have a wellbeing score lower than the general population leave us with one that is higher.

Homelessness can happen at any time and to anyone. When it happens to a young person it can affect them for the rest of their life. At least 103,000 young people in the UK are homeless right now and homeless young people are almost twice as likely to die as their non-homeless peers.

Every purchase of this book contributes to our funds and our ability to work with more young people in need.

Together we can make a difference.

Alex Eagle, Co-founder
www.therunningcharity.org

ACKNOWLEDGEMENTS

We would like to thank everyone who answered our appeal for their running stories. We received a larger and more diverse response than we could have wished for, testament surely to the importance running has for so many of us. The readiness to openly share personal experiences and feelings speaks volumes. To those whose stories have been selected, this is your book. To those whose stories did not make the cut this time, we are sorry we could not include all those we received. It was not an easy task to arrive at what we hope is a good and balanced selection.

Special thanks to Gigi Giannella for allowing us to use stories and images from his work; to Adrian Lobb for assiduously proofreading the text – any remaining errors are ours alone; to Teddy Page for arriving in the nick of time to so ably lead and co-ordinate our communications effort; to Martin Wright for wise counsel; and to Alex Eagle and the team at The Running Charity for lending their support to our endeavour.

Jerry Lockspeiser
Andrew Roberts

Jerry Lockspeiser is an entrepreneur, writer and business consultant. He took up running in his mid-50s after increasingly frequent injuries put an end to his football days. He has run 23 marathons, including the six Abbott Marathon Majors. Pleased to have set a marathon PB age 65, he remains in awe of Andrew's superior speed and age grading. Jerry is a Director of Positive News, fellow of the RSA, and qualified RAC motorcycle instructor. This is his third book.

Andrew Roberts is a freelance graphic designer who also shoots short videos. Occasionally he dresses up as an extra on movies. Most days after sedentary work he runs around London. His race range is from one mile to half marathon, but he prefers a local 5k to big events that combine running with queuing. He holds the UK mile record for his age group in 2015. Andrew admits to enjoying running past fit looking younger folk like Jerry.

Jerry and Andrew are members of the Serpentine Running Club in London. Andrew's photo is courtesy of Oleg Galimov and Sri Chimnoy Races.

Made in United States
Orlando, FL
13 March 2023